BEATS UNLEASHED

A JOURNEY INTO DRUMMING

**L'école Chempaka Society
for Educare**

notionpress.com

INDIA · SINGAPORE · MALAYSIA

ISBN 979-8-89929-733-5

About the Authors

 Anil G.T

A versatile drummer and passionate educator, Anil G.T hails from Trivandrum and was trained under the mentorship of Sri Suresh Daniel (Trivandrum), Sri Binil John Eapen (Muscat), Sri Joe Boy (Thrissur), and Sri Jeo Raj George (Bangalore).

Anil G.T is a seasoned drummer with over 32 years of experience, having performed alongside some of the most celebrated playback singers across multiple languages. A dedicated educator, he has spent two decades training students for the prestigious Trinity College London examinations, ensuring they receive high-quality music education.

Beyond his professional performances, Anil G.T has served as a drum instructor at reputed institutions, inspiring and mentoring countless students in their musical journey.

 Sreekumar R. Nair

A versatile musician and passionate educator, Sreekumar R. Nair hails from Trivandrum and was trained in Carnatic classical music under the mentorship of the late Sri Iraniyal Perumal (Classical Musician) and the late Smt. Annapoorna (Classical Musician). He has also received Western, Innovative & Contemporary music training from Sri Devissaro (Composer/Director, Australian Musician) and is currently learning Western violin under Sri Deepu, a disciple of Gleb Nechaev (Russian Violinist).

With over 25 years of experience, Sreekumar has built an illustrious career as a Singer, Actor, Composer, Teacher, and Trainer, showcasing his passion and expertise across multiple artistic disciplines.

He is a founding member of Asima Ensemble (Beyond Boundaries), a globally recognized music collective known for blending Indian classical and Hindustani music with world influences. As a multi-instrumentalist, he plays various percussion instruments, including the Djembe and Darbuka, demonstrating a deep understanding of rhythm and world music traditions.

His musical journey has taken him to some of the world's most prestigious venues and festivals, including: Haverhill Arts Centre, UK (2007), BBC Proms, Royal Albert Hall (2009), Kennedy Centre, USA (2011), Festival of Sacred Music, Thiruvaiyaru (2012), Asian Music Circuit, UK (2012), and Southbank Centre, London & China (2013).

Sreekumar has collaborated with internationally renowned artists such as George Brooks (USA - Saxophonist), Dhevdhas Nair (UK - Jazz Pianist), Eero Hämeenniemi (Finland - Composer), and Gleb Nechaev (Russia - Western Violinist), expanding his artistic reach across continents.

A dedicated educator, he served as Head of the Music Department at a reputed CBSE institution for over a decade and currently heads Chempaka Music Academy (L'école Chempaka Research and Training Centre, Trivandrum).

Beyond live performances and teaching, he has worked as a Music Content Manager for leading radio stations in Dubai, Bangalore, and Kerala, specializing in professional music software such as Powergold and RCS. He has also served as an A&R Manager for a leading audio company. At Chempaka Music Academy, he utilizes MuseScore 4 for writing notations, ensuring a structured and professional approach to music education.

Why Beats unleashed?

This Drum Textbook is the result of a collaborative effort between Anil G.T. and Sreekumar R. Nair, designed to serve as a comprehensive guide for drum enthusiasts, beginners, and students preparing for the Initial Grade & Grade 1 Trinity College London Examinations.

This book is an excellent resource for students who are just beginning their journey into the exciting world of drumming. Whether you're brand new or have already started playing, this guide will help you learn to **read, write, and understand drum notation** with ease.

Designed especially for young learners, this textbook introduces you to the **basics of music theory, note values, rhythmic patterns**, and **drum writing exercises** in a fun and simple way. Each lesson builds your confidence and skills, step by step.

The Chempaka Way in Music Education

At Chempaka Music Academy, "The Chempaka Way" is reflected in a structured yet flexible approach to music education. It ensures that students receive individual attention while fostering collaboration and artistic exploration.

Structured Learning

A well-defined curriculum aligned with Trinity College London ensures students develop strong technical skills.

Creative Expression

Beyond technical proficiency, students are encouraged to compose, improvise, and explore various musical styles.

Integration with Academics

Music is taught as a powerful learning tool, connecting with subjects like mathematics, language, and history.

Performance and Exposure

Students showcase their talents through concerts, assessments, and school events, building confidence and stage presence.

Community and Teamwork

Choirs, ensembles, and the formation of a school band create opportunities for collaboration and teamwork.

Vision

The Chempaka Music Academy Drumming Textbook aims to be a comprehensive and structured resource for aspiring drummers, providing a strong foundation in drumming techniques, rhythm development, and performance skills. Designed for learners of all levels, this textbook seeks to inspire and nurture a passion for drumming while integrating both traditional and contemporary drumming methods. Our goal is to empower students with the knowledge and confidence to explore their unique rhythmic abilities, embrace musical creativity, and excel in their drumming journey.

"Playing my drums is therapy."

Travis Barker

Chempaka Music Academy's Drums Textbook

Welcome to the Chempaka Music Academy, where music education meets passion and creativity. At Chempaka, we believe in nurturing talent and shaping the musical journey of each student with personalized attention, world-class instruction, and a curriculum that is both innovative and rooted in tradition. Our academy is dedicated to providing a high-quality musical education, creating an environment where students can explore, grow, and excel in their musical pursuits.

This **Drums Textbook Vol – 1** is designed to guide you through the essential skills and techniques required to master the drums, whether you're a beginner or an experienced player looking to refine your craft. With a structured approach and step-by-step lessons, these textbook covers everything from basic rhythms to advanced drumming techniques. The goal of this textbook is not just to teach you how to play the drums, but to help you develop a deep understanding of rhythm, coordination, and musical expression.

Through this book, you will learn about different drum techniques, including basic beats, hand-foot coordination, note durations, and much more, all while applying these skills in various musical contexts. Whether you aim to play in a school band, perform on stage, or simply explore the joy of drumming, this textbook will provide you with the foundation needed to unlock your full potential as a drummer.

We are excited to accompany you on this musical journey. Let's drum up some excitement and get started.

Importance of Learning Drums

Learning the drums offers a multitude of benefits that extend far beyond just the ability to play rhythms. As one of the most dynamic and expressive instruments, drumming plays a critical role in developing a student's musicality, coordination, and personal growth. At Chempaka Music Academy, we believe that drumming not only enhances musical skills but also nurtures qualities that are beneficial to a student's overall development.

Musical Benefits:

1. **Rhythmic Foundation**:
   Drums serve as the backbone of any musical ensemble, providing the **rhythm** that drives the music forward. By learning drums, students gain a deep understanding of **timing, rhythm, and beat**—critical elements in all forms of music. They learn to count, follow time signatures, and keep steady beats, building a strong foundation for other instruments or vocal performances.

2. **Coordination and Independence**:
   Drumming is one of the most challenging instruments when it comes to **coordination**. Drummers must learn to move their limbs independently—hands playing one rhythm, feet playing another. This helps improve **fine motor skills**, **hand-eye coordination**, and **bilateral coordination**, all of which are beneficial in other areas of life.

3. **Musical Expression**:
   The drum kit is an incredibly expressive instrument. Drummers can convey emotion and energy through dynamic control, accentuating the music with **powerful fills**, subtle ghost notes, and complex patterns. As students master these techniques, they learn to express themselves not just through playing notes, but through creating an emotional connection with the music.

4. **Improved Listening Skills**:
   Drummers must develop strong **listening skills** to stay in sync with the rest of the band or track. By learning to pay attention to nuances in rhythm, timing, and dynamics, drummers also enhance their ability to listen and respond musically in real-time.

Personal Benefits:

1. **Discipline and Focus**:
   Drumming requires **practice** and **concentration**. The process of learning new beats, sticking patterns, and complex rhythms instils a sense of discipline and attention to detail. Students quickly learn that consistent practice is key to progress, fostering perseverance and focus in both their musical and academic pursuits.

2. **Boosting Confidence**:
   The ability to master drumming techniques and perform with others boosts self-confidence and provides a sense of accomplishment. As students improve, they gain the courage to perform in front of others, whether in class, at a recital, or during a live performance.

3. **Stress Relief and Emotional Outlet**:
   Drumming is a powerful tool for **stress relief** and emotional expression. The physicality of drumming, combined with the focus required, can act as a healthy outlet for frustration, stress, and negative emotions. It allows students to channel their feelings into something positive, providing a cathartic and therapeutic experience.

4. **Creativity and Problem Solving**:
   Drummers are constantly challenged to create new rhythms, experiment with different sounds, and think critically about how to play their parts in various musical contexts. This enhances their **creativity** and **problem-solving skills**, helping them develop an innovative mindset that can be applied in other areas of life.

5. **Teamwork and Collaboration**:
   Drumming, especially in a band or group setting, teaches **teamwork** and the value of collaboration. Students learn how to listen to others, adjust their playing to fit the ensemble, and contribute to the overall sound. This fosters a sense of community and helps students develop interpersonal skills that are valuable in both their musical and personal lives

Conclusion

Learning the drums offers a wide array of benefits, from sharpening musical skills such as timing and rhythm to fostering personal growth in areas like focus, discipline, and self-expression. Whether as a standalone pursuit or as part of a musical ensemble, drumming provides students with a unique opportunity to develop in ways that are both musically enriching and personally transformative. At Chempaka Music Academy, we are committed to nurturing these qualities, empowering students to excel both in music and in life.

Introduction to the Drum Textbook

Welcome to the exciting world of **rhythm and percussion**.

This drum textbook is carefully designed to provide a **strong foundation** for young learners who are just beginning their musical journey. Whether you are a **complete beginner** at the Initial Grade level or a student moving forward into **Grade 1**, this book is the perfect companion to guide you every step of the way.

 **What's in it for me?**

1. **Step-by-Step Learning:** The book is structured in a clear, progressive manner, starting with the basics of drumming techniques, posture, and grip, and gradually introducing more complex rhythms and patterns.

2. **Beginner-Friendly Content:** Written with beginners in mind, the explanations are simple, concise, and easy to follow, ensuring that students can grasp concepts without feeling overwhelmed.

3. **Practical Exercises:** Each chapter includes practical exercises and practice routines to reinforce learning and help students develop muscle memory and timing.

4. **Visual Aids:** Diagrams, illustrations, and notation examples are provided to make learning more engaging and accessible.

5. **Foundation for Advanced Learning:** By mastering the fundamentals in this book, students will be well-prepared to tackle more advanced drumming techniques and styles in the future.

Important Points:

For those preparing for the Initial Grade and beyond in TCL, here are some important tips from Chempaka Music Academy. Kindly take note of the following points, as they will help you achieve a good score in the grading.

You may be proficient in reading and playing music, but that alone is not enough. Each piece is assessed based on fluency and accuracy, technical facility, communication and interpretation, improvisation, and musical knowledge.

Additionally, you should focus on technical work, aural skills, and sight-reading, as these areas will significantly contribute to your overall score in the examination.

The grading criteria are as follows:

- Pass: 60
- Merit: 75
- Distinction: 87

How to Use This Book

Welcome to your guide on how to make the most of the **Chempaka Music Academy Drums Textbook**. This book is carefully designed to provide students with a structured and engaging approach to learning the drums. Whether you're just starting your drumming journey or refining your skills, this guide will help you navigate the content and optimize your learning experience.

1. **Start with the Basics**:
   Begin by understanding the foundational concepts laid out in the early chapters of the book. These sections cover essential skills such as grip, posture, basic rhythms, and rudiments, which are crucial for building a solid drumming foundation. Don't rush through these – mastering the basics will make advanced techniques easier to grasp later.

2. **Follow the Step-by-Step Approach**:
   Each chapter is designed to be progressive, with lessons building on what you've learned in the previous section. As you progress, focus on one technique or concept at a time. Practice each lesson thoroughly before moving on to the next one. Remember, consistency and repetition are key to mastering the drums.

3. **Use the Exercises Effectively**:
   The textbook includes numerous exercises that target different aspects of drumming, such as hand-foot coordination, timing, and groove development. These exercises are designed to challenge you while helping you refine your skills. Be sure to follow the instructions for each exercise and take your time to practice at various speeds, starting slowly and gradually increasing tempo as you become more comfortable.

4. **Practice with a Metronome**:
   Rhythm and timing are essential to drumming. Throughout the book, you'll find exercises designed to be practiced with a **metronome**, a tool that helps you develop a consistent sense of timing. Begin each exercise slowly, and as you gain confidence, increase the tempo. The goal is to maintain steady and accurate timing, which is essential for all drumming.

5. **Take Notes and Reflect**:
   As you work through the lessons, take notes on important concepts, areas of improvement, and new techniques you've learned. Reflecting on your progress will not only keep you motivated but also help you identify areas that need more focus. Consider creating a practice log to track your practice sessions and improvements over time.

6. **Perform and Have Fun**:
   Remember that music is meant to be enjoyable! As you become comfortable with new rhythms, start experimenting by incorporating them into your own musical projects. Whether it's playing along with a track or performing for friends and family, practice performing in real-world scenarios to develop stage presence and musical confidence.

Enjoy the process, stay consistent, and remember that the key to becoming a great drummer lies in both your dedication and passion for music. Happy drumming!

"Most great records really start with the drums."
Billy Corgan

History of Drum Kit or Drum Set:

The drum kit, or drum set, is a collection of percussion instruments played by a single musician. It is one of the most iconic and versatile instruments in modern music, having evolved over centuries. Here's an overview of its history.

Early Roots of Percussion

- Ancient Percussion Instruments: The foundation of the drum kit lies in percussion instruments, which are among the oldest musical tools known to humanity. Cultures worldwide have used drums for rituals, communication, and music for thousands of years.

- Marching Bands and Orchestras (18th-19th Century): In Western music, military and marching bands featured various drums (e.g., snare drum, bass drum) and cymbals. These were played by multiple percussionists.

The Birth of the Drum Kit

Edward "Dee Dee" Chandler (b. c. 1866, New Orleans – d. 1925, New Orleans) was a legendary and almost mythological pioneer of the modern drum set.

- **Late 19th Century:** The first steps toward a drum kit came with the invention of the "drummer's chair" or "trap set," where a single player could handle multiple instruments.

- **Early Hardware Innovations:** The invention of the bass drum pedal in the 1890s (credited to William F. Ludwig and his brother, Theobald) allowed drummers to play the bass drum hands-free. This innovation was crucial in consolidating drums into a single playable set.

- Drummers began experimenting by arranging snare drums, bass drums, cymbals, and small percussion like woodblocks around themselves.

- **Vaudeville and Theatre:** Early drum kits gained popularity in Vaudeville performances, where drummers needed to create a variety of sounds to accompany silent films and live shows.

Development in Jazz (1920s-1930s)

- The drum kit became an essential part of the emerging jazz genre, which required a rhythmic backbone.

- **Swing Music:** Drummers like Gene Krupa helped popularize the hi-hat cymbal, an evolution of earlier "low boy" cymbals that were placed closer to the ground.

- **Kits of this era typically included:**

  A bass drum with a pedal.
  A snare drum.
  A pair of tom-toms.
  Cymbals (ride, crash, and hi-hats).
- Drummers began to develop sophisticated techniques, with the drum set taking on a more prominent musical role.

Modern Drum Kits (1940s-1960s)

- **Be-Bop Era (1940s):** Smaller drum kits became popular with jazz be-bop, emphasizing speed, improvisation, and intricate rhythms.

- **Rock 'n' Roll Revolution (1950s–1960s):** The rise of rock music led to louder, more robust drum kits. Drummers like Ringo Starr (*The Beatles*) and Keith Moon (*The Who*) brought attention to creative and dynamic drumming. Drum sizes increased, and additional tom-toms and cymbals were added to meet the demands of louder, more energetic music.

Technological Advancements (1970s-Present)

- **Electronic Drums (1970s–Present):** Companies like Roland and Simmons pioneered electronic drum kits, allowing drummers to produce a wide range of sounds and integrate with electronic music.
- **Custom Kits**: Modern drum kits come in various sizes and configurations, tailored to different genres such as jazz, rock, metal, and fusion.
- **Material Innovations:** Advances in drum shell and cymbal materials have improved durability, resonance, and sound quality.
- **Hybrid Kits:** Many drummers now combine acoustic and electronic drums to expand their sonic possibilities and versatility.

Cultural Impact

- Today, the drum kit is a central element in nearly all forms of modern music, from pop and rock to jazz, hip- hop, and EDM.

- Legendary drummers such as Buddy Rich, John Bonham, Neil Peart, and Sheila E. have elevated the drum kit to an instrument of virtuosity and creativity.

The performance.
The practice.

Table of Contents

Initial Grade

1. Introduction to the Drum Kit

The drum kit, also known as a drum set, is a versatile and dynamic percussion instrument commonly used in a variety of musical styles, from rock and pop to jazz and classical. A standard drum kit is a combination of drums, cymbals, and hardware designed to provide rhythmic and percussive support in a musical ensemble. Each component has a unique role, contributing to the overall sound and rhythm. Below is an introduction to the key components of a drum kit:

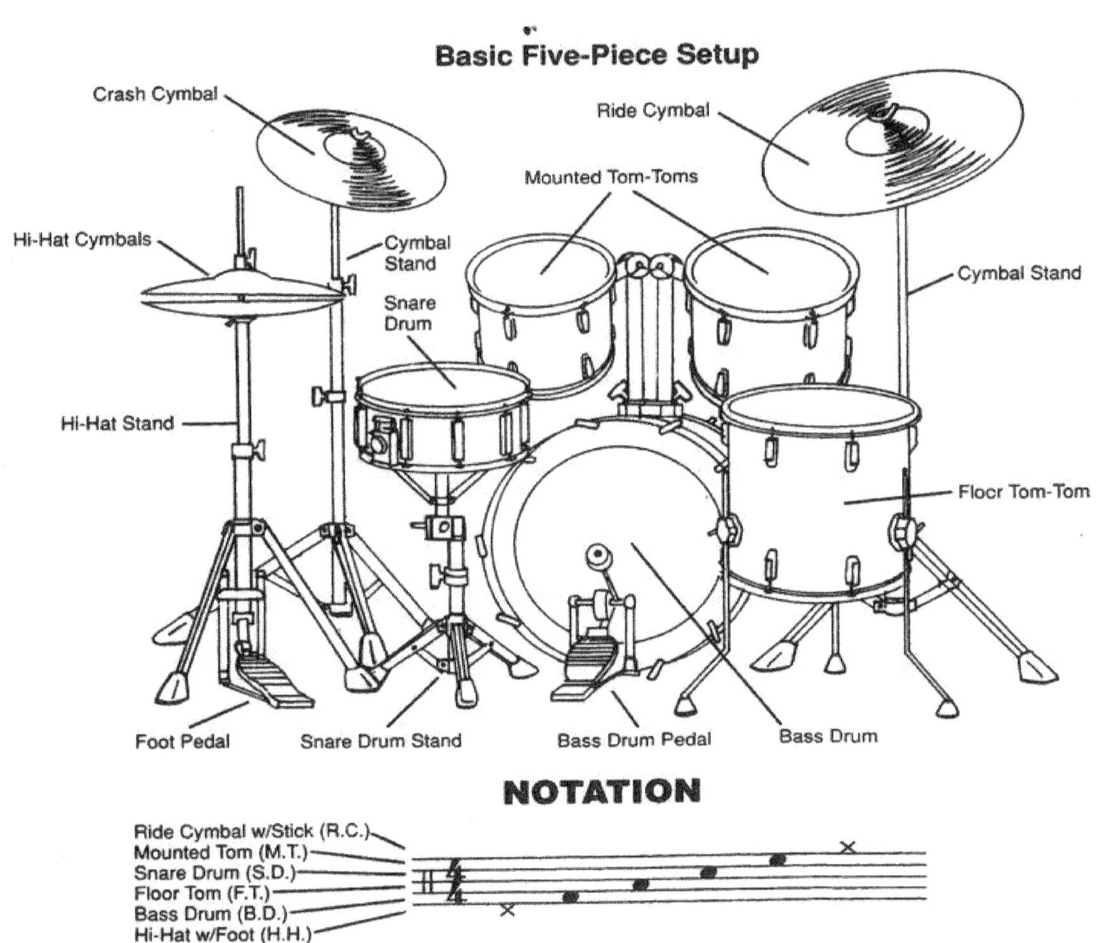

Bass Drum

The largest drum in the kit, also known as the kick drum. It produces deep, low-pitched beats and is typically played using a foot pedal. The bass drum serves as the foundation of the rhythm, often marking the primary beats in a measure.

Snare Drum

Positioned at the centre of the drum kit, the snare drum is characterized by its crisp and sharp sound. It has metal wires (snares) stretched across the bottom head, which create a distinctive "snap" when struck. It is a key element in creating grooves and backbeats.

Small Tom-Toms (1 & 2)

These are smaller drums mounted on top of the bass drum or a separate stand. They produce mid-range tones and are often used for fills and dynamic transitions between sections of a song.

Floor Tom-Tom

Larger than the small tom-toms, the floor tom produces a deeper, resonant tone. It is typically mounted on three legs and placed to the drummer's side, used for accentuating rhythms or dramatic effects.

Hi-Hat

A pair of cymbals mounted on a stand, controlled by a foot pedal. The hi-hat produces a variety of sounds, from tight, crisp "chicks" when closed to a shimmering sound when played open. It plays a crucial role in maintaining rhythm and dynamics.

Crash Cymbal

This cymbal produces a loud, explosive sound and is used for accents and transitions. It is commonly struck with drumsticks to emphasize significant moments in the music.

Ride Cymbal

Larger and heavier than the crash cymbal, the ride cymbal produces a sustained, "pinging" sound. It is often used to maintain a steady rhythm, especially in jazz and rock music.

Bass Drum Pedal

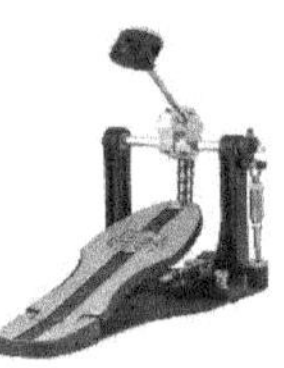

A foot-operated pedal used to strike the bass drum. It allows the drummer to maintain a consistent and controlled beat with the lower frequencies.

Matched Grip

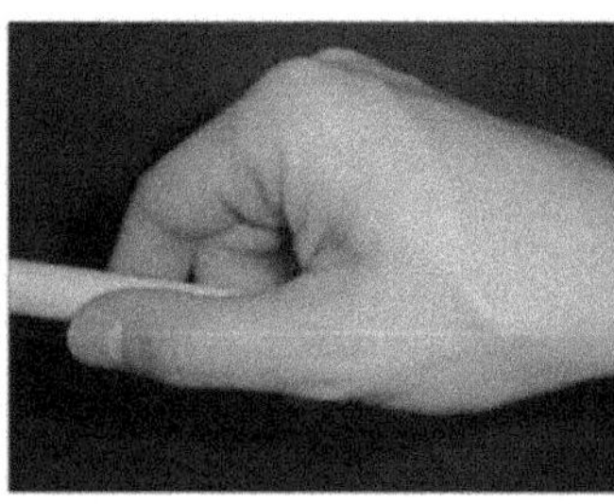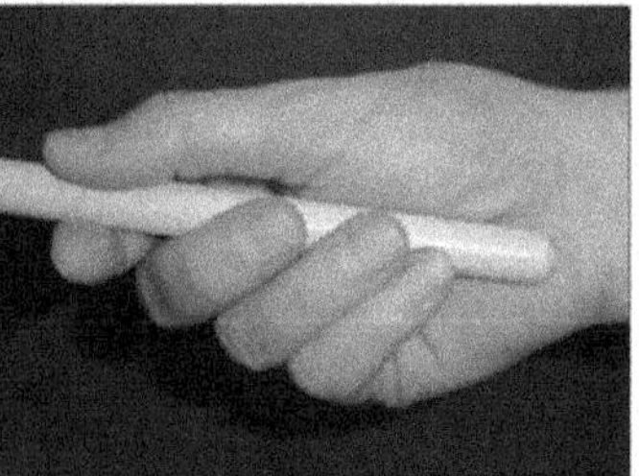

A widely used technique for holding drumsticks, where both hands hold the sticks in the same manner. This grip provides flexibility, balance, and control, making it suitable for a variety of drumming styles.

Materials Used in Drumstick Composition

Most drum sticks are wooden. Rosewood, maple, hickory and Japanese oak are the most popular woods used in the production of the sticks. Rosewood is dense hard wood while maple is light and soft. Hickory on the other hand is slightly harder as well as more durable than maple. In contrast, Japanese oak is extremely hard, durable and heavy. Apart from the wide spread wooden drum sticks, an individual may choose Carbon fiber, Ergonomic sticks, Plastic, Graphite, Fiber glass, Aluminum or light emitting diodes (LEDs) sticks that light up upon impact. It is also possible to choose a signature stick which is specifically designed to an individual's specifications.

Rosewood, Maple, Hickory, Japanese Oak

Basic Drumstick Parts (Tip, Shoulder, Shaft, Butt)

Despite the fact that drum sticks come in various sizes, weights and balances, all of them have similar basic designs. These features are the shoulder (tapered area), tip (which beats the drum head), butt (bottom end), and shaft (straight area which the hand holds). The shoulder can be extremely severe on heavier sticks or gradual on lighter ones.

The round, olive, barrel and pointed tip sticks are the most popular drum sticks in the market. The olive tip provides complete, low tones and enhanced durability, the round is bright and focused, both the barrel and pointed tips provide a medium tone. However, the barrel tip has more focus because of its reduced contact area.

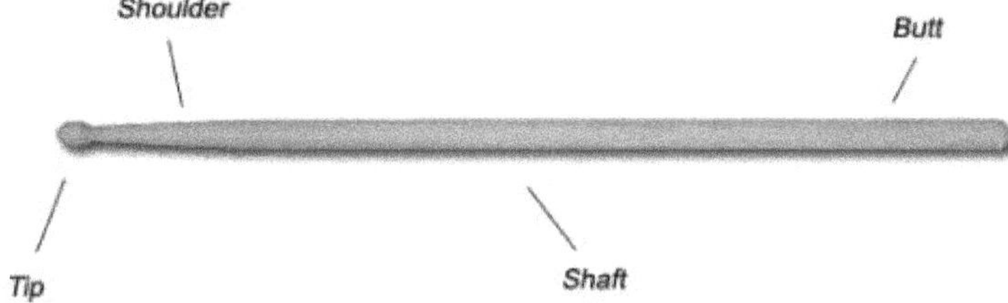

Stick Size Nomenclature

Although the drum stick sizes may vary from one manufacturer to another, the international accepted drum stick numbering system devised in the 20th century provides the buyer with a rough idea of what to purchase. Generally, there are three categories denoted by letter S, A and B.

The notation **A** stands for **orchestra**, **B** for **band** and **S** for **street**. Class A is the lightest and was primarily designed for large bands while B was originally designed for brass and symphonic bands. The third category, S means street and was designed as the largest as well as heaviest drum stick in the market. The street uses incorporated drum corps plus marching bands designs. The accompanying digits refer to the circumference of the drum stick. The common numbers are two, five and seven. The larger the digit, the smaller the circumference of the drum sticks.

Five A are the most popular and appropriate drum sticks for standard beginners. However, 7A is ideal for young drummers who need a lighter drum stick. Experienced and hardcore drummers, who want to beat the drum hard, may try a 2B or 5B. Hopefully we have given you an interesting insight and now you have some idea of what to consider when choosing drum stick sizes.

- **The Neck**

The neck is the thinnest point of the entire drumstick. Thicker stick necks are more durable and likely to make your stick last longer, but this can make the stick feel clunky and unresponsive. There was a time when drumstick necks would break regularly and the drumstick tips would just fly off, but the reliability of drumsticks has improved greatly over the years.

- **The Taper**

The taper is where the stick thickens and widens, from the neck all the way up to the shoulder of the stick. The design of this part of the stick has a big impact on the playability of the stick, giving a stick part of its unique feel when you strike the drum. Sticks that are thinner and longer are often described as highly responsive sticks. Heavier and shorter sticks provide more power, but are stiffer and harder in the hands. A shorter taper will favor a drummer who prefers to have more power and a longer taper will favor a drummer who prefers responsiveness. There's no right answer when it comes to choosing a style of taper that you like.

- **The Shoulder**

The shoulder of the stick can be found at the end of the taper, where the taper has reached its thickest point. The location of the shoulder is determined by how long the taper is. So, the longer a taper is, the further away from the tip the shoulder is. The shorter the taper is, the closer the shoulder is to the tip. This part of the stick is mostly used for a single drum technique, which is to "crash" a cymbal. Rather than playing on the top of a cymbal with the tip, we can get a much warmer and washier sound by striking the side of the cymbal with the shoulder of the stick.

Tip: When "crashing the cymbal with the shoulder of the stick, make sure to avoid hitting the edge of the cymbal at too sharp an angle.

The stick should never be at 90 degrees like this. Your drumstick (or cymba) is likely to break very quickly.

Here's how your stick should look as you strike the cymbal with the shoulder.

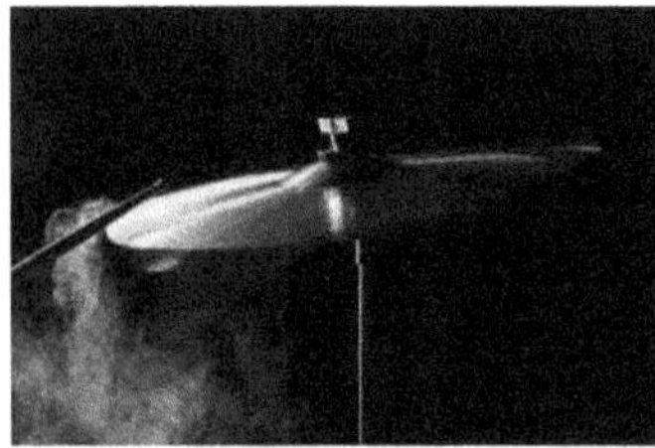

Hitting the crash with the shoulder of the stick. The tip of the stick never touches the cymbal, only the shoulder.

- ## The Shaft/Body

The shaft or body is the main thick section that provides most of the weight to the drumstick. The thickness and weight of this area will have a big impact on how the stick feels to play. Thicker sticks, such as 2Bs and 5Bs, will deliver a huge amount of power thanks to their increased weight, but can be difficult to move around the kit. Lighter sticks, such as 7As, are great for more complex and intricate drumming, but deliver less power. There are two occasions in which the shaft of the stick comes into contact with the drum. The first is when using the cross-stick technique (shown below) which creates a rim-clicking sound, popular in jazz, ballads and music that requires less volume.

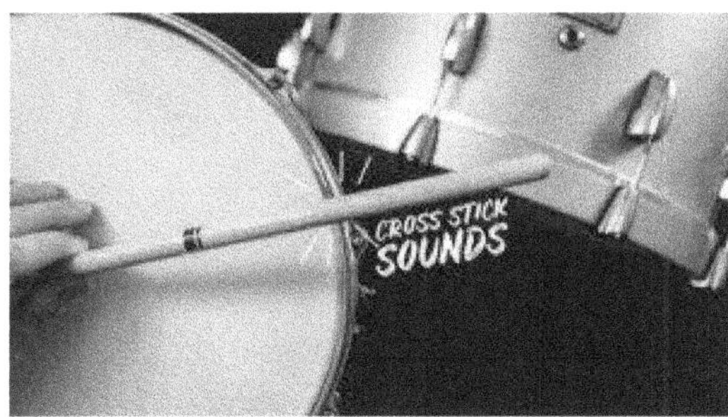

cross stick snare drum hit

In the cross-stick technique, the stick is turned around the opposite way to play. The tip of the stick sits in the center of the drum; the drummer then controls the stick with a light grip to knock the body/shaft against the rim. The other time that you would play with the body of the stick would be when playing a rimshot.

snare drum rimshot

When playing a rimshot, you strike the center of the drum and the rim of the drum simultaneously. This creates a much more powerful and defined sound, ideal for rock, metal and any genre that requires a punchier style of drumming.

- ## The Butt

The final area of the stick is the butt end, where we will be holding the stick most of the time. There's no defined point at which the body of the stick becomes the butt, but we just think of the butt as the end of the stick that is the thickest.

Drummer's will turn their sticks around to play with the butt end instead of the tip, to get a heavier, fuller sound. Adding a rimshot to the mix as well as using the butt. They use the shaft of the stick on the rim while using the butt end to play the center of the drum. This creates a truly earth-shaking sound; it delivers even more power for drummers that need to be heard in the noisiest musical situations.

The most important part of a drumstick is the tip.

Different Drumstick Tips

Drum companies are always designing new variations for drumstick tips, however, most typically fall into a number of popular categories:

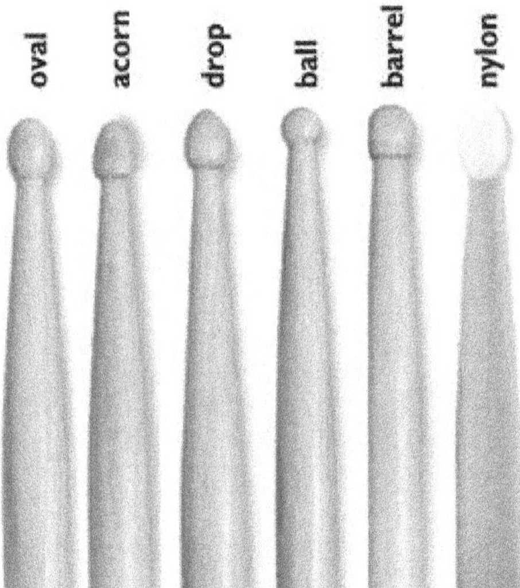

Types of drum stick tips

- **Ball**: A ball shaped tip is a useful tip shape because it provides incredible consistency to your playing. The tone you produce with this stick tip is likely to be very even and well-balanced. Because the amount of surface area that comes into contact with the drum you are playing is always the same. This is because it has a perfect sphere shape (shown above), so whatever angle you hit the drum at, you'll get the same amount of stick surface area coming into contact with the drum. The ball shape provides a bright, light and crisp sound.

- **Oval:** The oval tip is a really expressive stick shape, providing great variety in tone to the drummer who plays with them. In contrast to tips like the ball shape, you have a lot of freedom with the sound you choose to generate every time you sit down to play. You can play your drums at different angles to change up your tone pretty easily with this stick. If you're not sure what tone you like, try an oval stick. You'll have access to a wider range of overtones with this stick.

- **Acorn:** Acorn tips typically have a large surface area that comes into contact with the drum. This produces a fuller, fatter sound with a nice rounded mix of tones. The acorn tip is a heavy lifter in the world of drumstick tips, and it's well worth having a pair of acorn tips in your stick bag. The acorn tip is versatile enough to suit most musical styles and genres.

- **Drop/Teardrop:** You'll find this shape on the most popular drumsticks ever created (the Vic Firth's American Classic 5As), and it's easy to understand why. Like the acorn tip, it has a large surface area coming into contact with the drum, providing a warm, full and highly desirable tone. Like the acorn, you can use the teardrop in many musical situations, making it another top all-round choice. So, if you're a fan of the teardrop shape but need a stick with a big more oomph for loud musical settings, you could choose a 5B stick over a 5A stick.

- **Barrel:** The barrel tip is small and fat. It provides a punchy sound favored by some of the world's top drummers. The barrel tip is great for producing a high-quality recording sound in the studio.

- **Nylon:** Nylon tips produce a brighter sound than wood sticks on average for stick tips of the same size. In particular, they are able to generate a sharp 'ping' sound from playing the cymbals. This can help drummers be heard more clearly, particularly when playing in noisy environments. Nylon tips also tend to break less easily and don't wear down like wood tips do.

Drumstick Size

Vic Firth is the most popular drumstick maker in the world. Listed below are Vic Firth drumstick sizes.

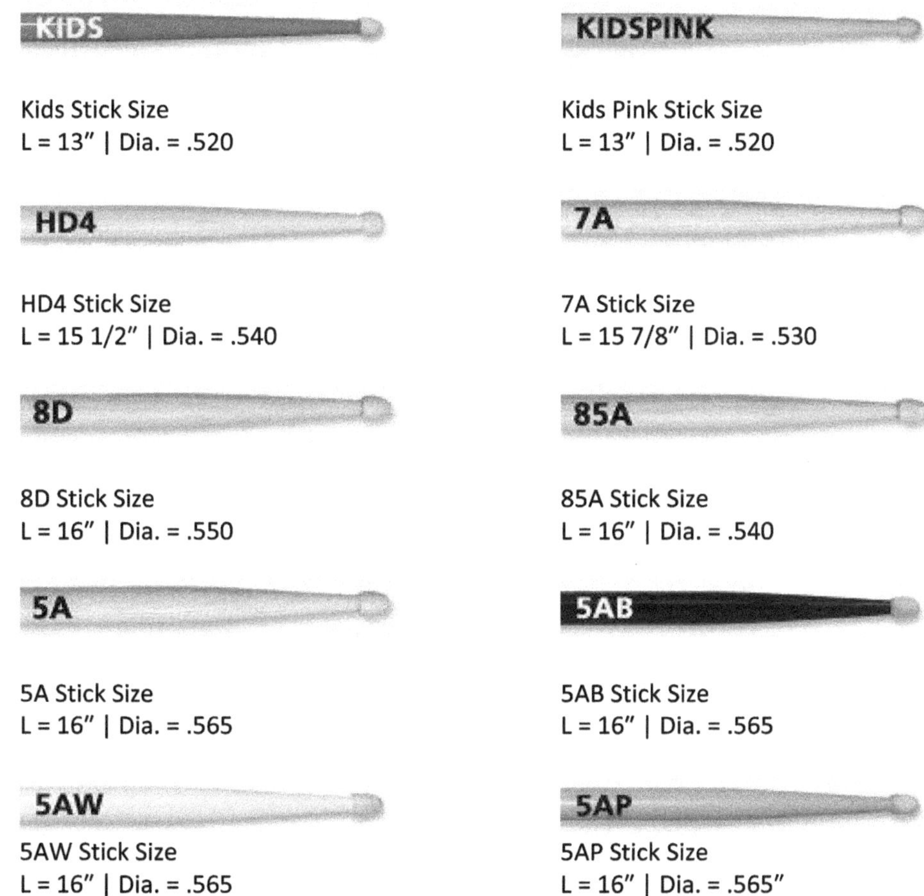

Kids Stick Size
L = 13" | Dia. = .520

Kids Pink Stick Size
L = 13" | Dia. = .520

HD4 Stick Size
L = 15 1/2" | Dia. = .540

7A Stick Size
L = 15 7/8" | Dia. = .530

8D Stick Size
L = 16" | Dia. = .550

85A Stick Size
L = 16" | Dia. = .540

5A Stick Size
L = 16" | Dia. = .565

5AB Stick Size
L = 16" | Dia. = .565

5AW Stick Size
L = 16" | Dia. = .565

5AP Stick Size
L = 16" | Dia. = .565"

5ADT

5ADT Stick Size
L = 16 1/2" | Dia. = .565

X5A

X5A Stick Size
L = 16 1/8" | Dia. = .565

55A

55A Stick Size
L = 16" | Dia. = .595

5B

5B Stick Size
L = 16" | Dia. = .580

5BB

5BB Stick Size
L = 16" | Dia. = .595

5BW

5BW Stick Size
L = 16" | Dia. = .595

5BCO

5BCO Stick Size
L = 16 1/2" | Dia. = .595

X5B

X5B Stick Size
L = 16 1/4" | Dia. = .595

F1

F1 Stick Size
L = 16 3/16" | Dia. = .580

3A

3A Stick Size
L = 16 3/16" | Dia. = .580

1A

1A Stick Size
L = 16 1/4" | Dia. = .610

HD9

HD9 Stick Size
L = 16 13/16" | Dia. = .580

2B

2B Stick Size
L = 16 5/8" | Dia. = .630

ROCK

ROCK Stick Size
L = 16 1/4" | Dia. = .630

CM

CM Stick Size
L = 16 1/2" | Dia. = .563

ESTICK

ESTICK Stick Size
L = 17" | Dia. = .635

2. Time Signature

In music, a **time signature** is a crucial notation that indicates how the rhythm of a piece is structured. It tells the drummer how many beats are in each measure (or bar) and what type of note receives one beat. Time signatures are written at the beginning of a musical piece, just after the clef and key signature, and are represented as two numbers stacked vertically, like a fraction.

Understanding Time Signatures

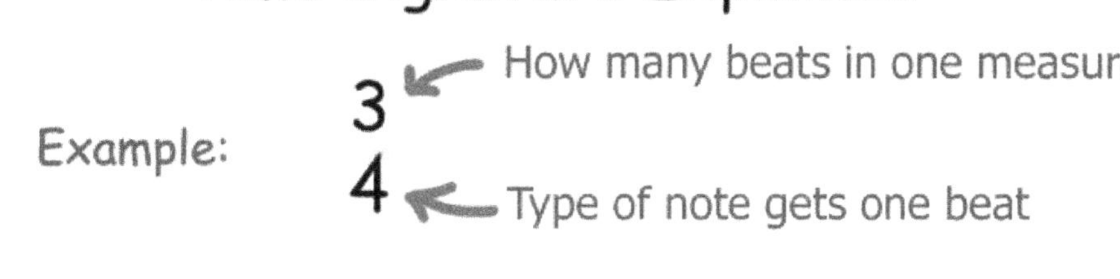

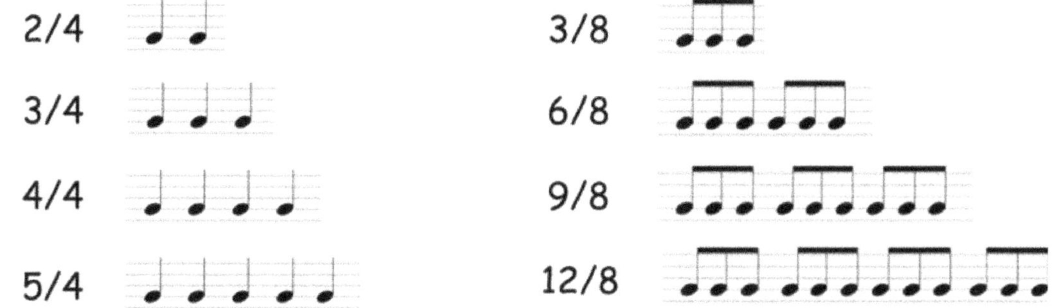

A. The Top Number

This indicates the number of beats in each measure. For example:

- A "4" means there are **4 beats per measure**.
- A "3" means there are **3 beats per measure**.
- A "6" indicates **6 beats per measure**, often grouped into smaller units.

B. The Bottom Number

This indicates the type of note that receives one beat:

- A "4" represents a **quarter note**.
- An "8" represents an **eighth note**.
- A "2" represents a **half note**.

Common Time Signatures

4/4 (Common Time)

Known as "common time," this is the most widely used time signature. It means there are 4 beats per measure, and the quarter note gets one beat.
Example: **1-2-3-4 (repeat)**

3/4 (Waltz Time)

Used in waltzes and other dances, it has 3 beats per measure, with the quarter note receiving one beat.
Example: **1-2-3 (repeat)**

6/8 (Compound Time)

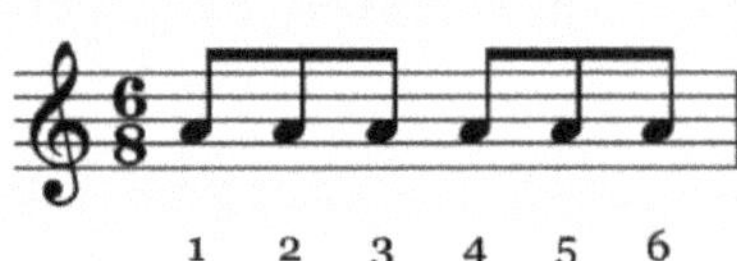

A compound time signature with 6 beats per measure, often grouped into two sets of three beats. The eighth note receives one beat.
Example: **1-2-3, 4-5-6**

2/4 (March Time)

Often found in marches, it has 2 beats per measure, and the quarter note gets one beat.
Example: **1-2 (repeat)**

<u>How Time Signatures Guide Drummers</u>

For drummers, understanding time signatures is essential to playing rhythms accurately and keeping the band in sync. The time signature helps you decide:

- The number of beats to count in each measure.

- The placement of accents, fills, and dynamics.

- The rhythm pattern to follow for specific styles of music.

For example:

- In **4/4 time**, you might play a basic rock beat with a steady bass drum on beats 1 and 3, and a snare drum on beats 2 and 4.

- In **3/4 time**, you could emphasize the first beat to create a waltz-like feel.

Practicing Time Signatures

- Start by clapping or tapping the beats while counting aloud.

- Practice simple drum patterns in each time signature.

- Gradually add complexity with fills and dynamics.

- Play along with songs to develop a natural feel for various time signatures.

By mastering time signatures, drummers can confidently navigate different musical styles and provide a strong rhythmic foundation for any ensemble.

3. Time Value

Time value refers to the duration of a note or rest in music, which determines how long it is played or remains silent. In drumming, understanding time value is essential for maintaining rhythm, creating dynamic patterns, and synchronizing with other musicians. Notes and rests are measured relative to the beat, and their values are defined by the time signature of the music.

Note Durations

Additionally, sixteenth notes are usually grouped together to make 1 beat as well. Since they are ¼ beat a piece, they are grouped in sets of 4.

Make sense? So, let's see the big picture!

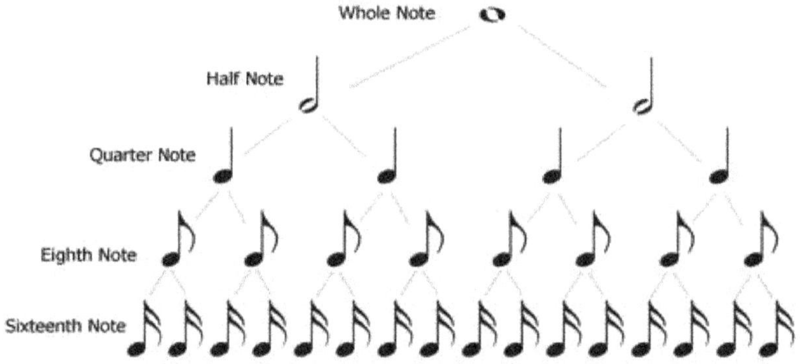

Whole Note

The longest note value in common time.
Duration: **4 beats** in a 4/4-time signature.
On drums: Often represented by a sustained crash cymbal or an extended pause.

Half Note

Half the length of a whole note.
Duration: **2 beats** in a 4/4-time signature.
On drums: Typically used in slower rhythms or accents on cymbals.

Quarter Note

A fundamental unit of rhythm.
Duration: **1 beat** in a 4/4-time signature.
On drums: Commonly used for steady beats on the bass drum or hi-hat.

Eighth Note

Half the length of a quarter note.
Duration: **1/2 beat** in a 4/4-time signature.
On drums: Often used for faster hi-hat patterns or rolls.

Sixteenth Note

Half the length of an eighth note.
Duration: **1/4 beat** in a 4/4-time signature.
On drums: Frequently used for intricate fills or rapid snare rolls.

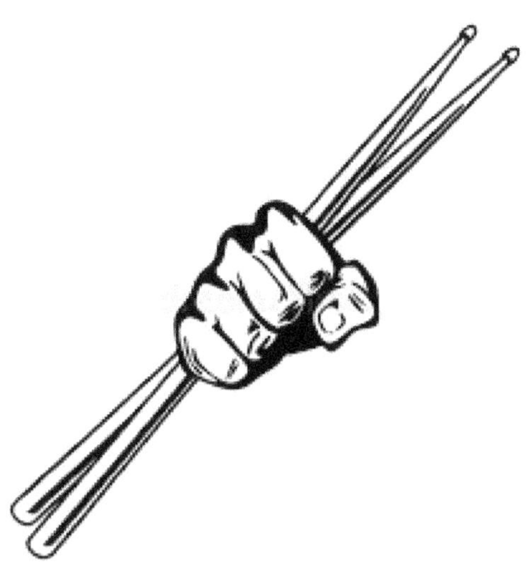

<u>Rest Durations</u>

Rests represent periods of silence and are equally important in creating dynamic and rhythmic variety in drumming.

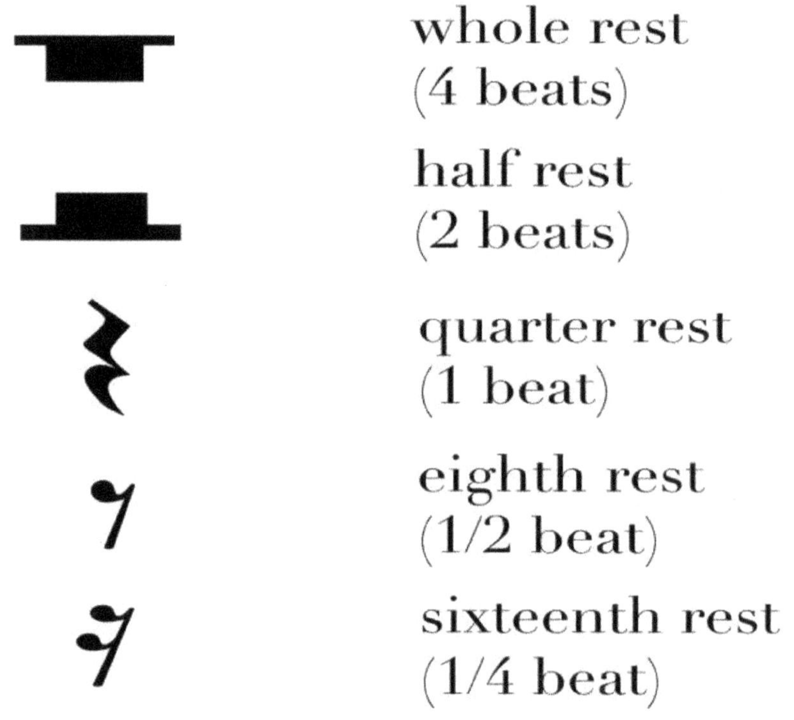

Whole Rest

Silence for **4 beats**.
Often used between sections of a song.

Half Rest

Silence for **2 beats**.
Creates pauses within phrases.

Quarter Rest

Silence for **1 beat**.
Used to punctuate rhythms.

Eighth Rest

Silence for **1/2 beat**.
Adds syncopation and variety to patterns.

Sixteenth Rest

Silence for **1/4 beat**.
Useful for complex, rapid rhythms.

Understanding Time Value on the Drum Kit

Time values are not about sustaining sounds (as on other instruments) but about when and how drums and cymbals are struck.

Each time value corresponds to a specific moment in the rhythm, helping to create patterns and fills.

Practical Applications for Drummers

Keeping Steady Beats

Use quarter notes on the hi-hat or ride cymbal to maintain a steady rhythm.

Creating Syncopation

Combine eighth notes, rests, and sixteenth notes for more complex, off-beat patterns.

Fills and Transitions

Utilize a mix of note values for dynamic fills that lead smoothly between song sections.

Dynamic Expression

Use longer rests for dramatic pauses and shorter notes for fast-paced, energetic passages.

Practice Exercises

- **Clapping and Counting**

Clap each note duration while counting aloud. For example, in 4/4 time:

Whole Note: "1-2-3-4"
Half Notes: "1-2, 3-4"
Quarter Notes: "1, 2, 3, 4"

- **Playing on the Drum Kit**

Practice quarter notes on the bass drum, eighth notes on the hi-hat, and sixteenth notes on the snare to build coordination.

- **Combine Notes and Rests**

Create simple rhythms using a mix of notes and rests to understand their relationship.

"Drums were my first instrument, my first love. I need rhythm, something that moves."
Patrick Stump

4. Semibreve - (Whole Note)

The semibreve, also known as a whole note, is one of the longest note values in music. It holds a duration of **four beats** in standard 4/4 time.

Characteristics of a Semibreve:

- **Symbol**: A hollow oval note head with no stem.

- **Duration**: Equivalent to four quarter notes or two half notes.

- **Rhythmic Function**: Used to sustain a single note or rest for an entire measure, creating a sense

  of space and stability in the rhythm.

Application in Drumming:

- In drum notation, a semibreve is often represented on the **ride cymbal, hi-hat**, or as a single hit on a **bass drum** or **snare**, depending on the desired texture.

- It's commonly used in slow-tempo pieces, where it allows the drummer to hold a steady groove while other instruments fill the space.

Practice Tip:

- Play a steady **4/4 beat**, using the semibreve on the ride cymbal. Focus on maintaining even spacing between each beat to develop consistency and timing.

- Combine it with a steady **kick** and **snare** pattern to explore its role in various grooves.

5. Minim - (Half Note)

The minim, also known as a half note, has a duration of **two beats** in standard 4/4 time. It's a versatile note value that serves as a bridge between longer and shorter rhythms, creating a balanced and steady pulse.

Characteristics of a Minim:

- **Symbol**: A hollow oval note head with a vertical stem.

- **Duration**: Equivalent to two quarter notes or half of a semibreve.

- **Rhythmic Function**: Adds a sense of continuity and flow within a measure while allowing space for other rhythmic elements.

Application in Drumming:

- In drum notation, the minim is often used for **sustained cymbal hits**, **drum fills**, or **marking key beats** within a groove.

- It is ideal for slower tempos or sections that require a deliberate and steady rhythm.

Practical Exercises:

- **Basic Groove**: Use a minim on the ride cymbal or hi-hat to play on beats 1 and 3 while keeping the kick and snare steady on beats 1, 2, 3, and 4.

- **Drum Fills**: Incorporate minim hits on the toms or crash cymbals to add dynamic variation to your playing.

- **Timing Practice**: Set a metronome at a slow tempo and play minims evenly across the measure to develop accuracy and control.

6. Crotchet - (Quarter Note)

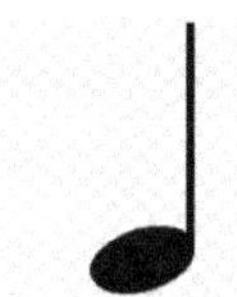

The **crotchet**, also known as a **quarter note**, is one of the most fundamental rhythmic values in music. It is the building block of countless drum patterns, serving as the backbone of timing and rhythm in most musical styles.

Characteristics of a Crotchet

- **Symbol**: A filled-in note head with a vertical stem.

- **Duration**: Lasts for **one beat** in standard 4/4 time.

- **Role in Rhythm**: Provides a steady and consistent pulse, forming the framework for other note values.

Crotchet in Drumming

In drum notation, the crotchet is widely used for beats and grooves. Drummers use it to establish the tempo and create a strong, recognizable rhythm.

Common Applications:

- **Steady Pulse**: Played on the **hi-hat**, **ride cymbal**, or **snare drum** to maintain a consistent beat.

- **Kick and Snare Patterns**: Often combined with other note values to create basic drum grooves.

- **Accents**: Used for marking key beats in a bar, especially on beats **1, 2, 3,** and **4** in 4/4 time.

Practical Exercises

- **Basic Groove**
Play crotchets on the hi-hat while alternating the kick on beat 1 and the snare on beat 3.

- **Timing Practice**
Set a metronome at a moderate tempo. Play crotchets evenly on the ride cymbal or snare to develop precision and control.

- **Dynamic Variations**
Experiment with playing crotchets softly or loudly to add dynamics to your drumming.

Why Master the Crotchet?

- It forms the foundation of drum grooves and patterns.
- It helps drummers lock in with other instruments, especially in ensemble playing.
- It enhances timing and tempo awareness, crucial for every drummer.

7. Drum Kit Notation Key

Understanding the **drum kit notation key** is essential for reading and playing drum music. It provides a visual map of how the various drums and cymbals are represented on a musical staff. By mastering this notation, drummers can accurately interpret rhythms, grooves, and fills across different styles of music.

The Drum Kit Notation Staff

Standard Staff: Drum notation is written on a five-line staff, similar to traditional music notation.

No Pitched Notes: Unlike other instruments, drum notation does not use pitch; each line or space represents a specific part of the drum kit.

Notation Key for Common Drum Kit Components:

- **Hi-Hat with Foot**
Written below the staff with a "x" symbol.

- **Bass Drum (Kick)**
Written on the bottom space with a regular note head.

- **Floor Tom**: Written on the fourth space.

- **Snare Drum**
Written on the third space with a regular note head.

- **Tom 2**
High Tom: written on the third space or line above the snare on the staff, depending on the notation system being used.

- **Tom 1**
Mid Tom: written on the third line of the staff, placed above the snare drum in drum notation.

- **Cymbals**
Ride Cymbal: Written on the top line or above the staff with an "x" note head.

Hi-Hat (Closed): Written on the top line with an "x" note head.

- **Crash Cymbal**: Written above the staff with an "x" note head.

- **Hi-Hat (Open)**: Same position as closed hi-hat, with an "o" above the note.

Other Percussion

- **Cowbell**: Typically written above the ride cymbal line.

- **Tambourine or Auxiliary Instruments**: Specific placement varies but is often labelled in the score.

How to Use the Drum Kit Notation Key

- **Quick Reference**: The key acts as a guide, especially for beginners learning to read drum scores.

- **Consistency**: Ensures players interpret drum parts the same way, regardless of the music's complexity.

- **Versatility**: Once familiar, drummers can easily adapt to various styles, from rock and jazz to pop and funk.

Practical Exercise

- **Memorization**: Practice identifying each part of the drum kit on the staff using a notation chart.

- **Simple Patterns**: Play basic grooves while referring to the notation key, gradually building speed and accuracy.

- **Advanced Practice**: Try reading full drum scores, using the notation key to decipher complex rhythms.

8. Crotchet Note Rest - (Quarter Note Rest)

The **crotchet rest**, also known as a **quarter note rest**, represents a period of silence lasting for **one beat** in standard 4/4 time. Just as the crotchet (quarter note) is used to represent a single, sustained sound, the crotchet rest is used to indicate a single, sustained silence, allowing space and breathing room within the rhythm.

Characteristics of the Crotchet Rest

- **Symbol**: A squiggly line resembling a "Z" shape, placed on the staff.

- **Duration**: Lasts for **one beat**, equal in length to a crotchet (quarter note).

- **Role in Rhythm**: The crotchet rest adds dynamics and timing to music, emphasizing where the drummer should **remain silent** while still maintaining the overall pulse.

- ### Crotchet Rest in Drumming

In drumming, rests are as important as the notes themselves, contributing to the overall rhythm and feel of a piece. The crotchet rest indicates a **brief pause** or **break** in the rhythm, and drummers must be mindful of when to rest and when to play, as it helps shape the musical flow.

- ### Common Applications:

Groove Variations: Incorporating rests in a groove can make the rhythm feel more dynamic and interesting by creating space between beats.

Drum Fills: Rests can be used in between drum fills to create tension before returning to the main rhythm.

Syncopation: The crotchet rest can be strategically placed to produce syncopated rhythms, making the music more lively and engaging.

Practical Exercises

- **Simple Rest Pattern**

    Play a basic 4/4 groove, with a **crotchet rest** on beat 2. This will help you practice controlling silence and rhythm.

    Example: Kick on beats 1 and 3, Snare on beat 4, and Hi-Hat on all beats except beat 2 (where the rest occurs).

- **Groove with Rests**

    Practice drumming on a groove with **crotchet rests** incorporated in different parts of the pattern to create interesting breaks and emphasize certain beats.

- **Silent Practice**

    Without the drum kit, clap your hands to the rhythm of a piece, incorporating **crotchet rests** to feel where the rests naturally occur and how they influence the overall rhythm.

Why Master the Crotchet Rest?

- **Rhythmic Precision**: Mastery of rests helps drummers play more complex rhythms and timings, adding sophistication to their performance.

- **Dynamics**: Resting at the right moments adds contrast, making the music more expressive.

- **Timing and Control**: Learning where and when to rest helps develop a stronger sense of rhythm and timing.

"Any sound, if it's in time, has some value."
– Benny Greb

9. Quaver – (Eighth Note)

The **quaver**, also known as an **eighth note**, is a fundamental note value in music that represents a sound lasting for **half a beat** in 4/4 time. It is one of the most commonly used note values in drumming, forming the foundation for many rhythmic patterns and grooves. Quavers add movement, speed, and energy to a piece of music, providing the necessary pulse to drive a rhythm forward.

Characteristics of the Quaver

- **Symbol**: A filled-in note head with a stem and a single flag attached to it.

- **Duration**: Lasts for **half a beat** in standard 4/4 time, meaning two quavers fit into the duration of one crotchet (quarter note).

- **Role in Rhythm**: Quavers are commonly used to subdivide beats into smaller, more detailed rhythmic values. They help to create fast-paced grooves, intricate drum patterns, and more complex rhythms.

Quaver in Drumming

In drumming, quavers are frequently used in faster patterns and fills. They allow drummers to play more notes within a single beat, giving music its sense of speed and movement. Quavers are essential for creating **smooth, continuous grooves**, and they often appear in combinations with other note values to build complex rhythms.

Common Applications:

Hi-Hat Patterns: Quavers are often played on the hi-hat to add a flowing rhythm, for example, playing quavers on every beat in a 4/4 measure.

Syncopation: Combining quavers with rests or other note values creates syncopated rhythms, where the beat feels off or delayed, adding interest to the music.

Fill Accents: Quavers can be used in fast fills between drum kit elements like toms, snare, and bass drum to provide quick, sharp movements.

Practical Exercises:

- **Basic Hi-Hat Practice**

Play quavers on the hi-hat in a steady 4/4 time, focusing on evenly spaced hits on each beat (1& 2& 3& 4&). This exercise helps with timing and consistency.

- **Snare and Kick with Quavers**

Try playing quavers on the snare drum while alternating kick drum hits on beats 1 and 3. Example: Snare on 1& 2& 3& 4&, Kick on 1 and 3.

Quaver Drum Fills

Practice a drum fill using quavers across all the toms, snare, and kick. Focus on maintaining even timing for each hit to develop speed and accuracy.

Why Master the Quaver?

- **Speed and Precision**: Learning the quaver allows drummers to play faster rhythms and execute complex fills with accuracy.

- **Groove Development**: Quavers are essential for creating energetic and smooth grooves, adding drive to the music.

- **Timing and Control**: Playing quavers forces you to be precise with your timing, helping develop a strong sense of rhythm and control over your playing.

"You only get better by playing.
If you think you stink, you probably do.
I consider every drummer that ever played before me an influence, in
every way."
- Buddy Rich

10.Single Stroke Roll

The **Single Stroke Roll** is one of the most fundamental and widely used rudiments in drumming. It consists of alternating single strokes between both hands (right and left), making it an essential technique for drummers of all levels. The Single Stroke Roll is the foundation for many advanced drumming techniques and provides the speed and fluidity needed to play complex rhythms and fills.

Characteristics of the Single Stroke Roll

- **Notation**: Each stroke is represented by a note head (either a filled or open note) followed by an alternating stick (right or left).

- **Duration**: Played continuously with alternating strokes (right, left, right, left) for a set number of beats or for as long as needed in the piece.

- **Role in Rhythm**: The Single Stroke Roll is used to create smooth, flowing rhythms and is commonly used in drum solos, drumlines, and fills. It develops the coordination between both hands, enhancing the overall fluidity and speed of the drummer's playing.

How to Play the Single Stroke Roll

Hand Alternation: Start by playing a **right-hand stroke (R)** followed by a **left-hand stroke (L)**. This should be done continuously, alternating between both hands.

Even Strokes: Aim to play each stroke with an even amount of force, producing a balanced sound from both hands.

Relaxed Grip: Keep your grip relaxed to avoid tension, which could slow down your playing. Focus on clean, controlled movements.

Stick Height: Make sure the height of your stick rebound is consistent for each stroke to maintain an even flow.

Practical Exercises

Slow and Steady

Start by playing the Single Stroke Roll at a slow tempo. Focus on accuracy and evenness between the right and left hand. Use a metronome to keep a consistent tempo.

Example: Play the roll for one or two measures, alternating right and left hands at a slow pace to build control.

Increase Speed Gradually

Once comfortable at a slower tempo, gradually increase the speed while maintaining evenness in your strokes.

Try to play the Single Stroke Roll faster without sacrificing control or clarity in each stroke.

Accent Practice

Practice adding accents to the roll to improve dynamic control. Play some strokes louder (accents) and others softer, creating a more dynamic and expressive sound.

Example: Accent every 3rd stroke, and continue alternating between the right and left hands.

Use with Drum Kit

Apply the Single Stroke Roll in basic drum patterns and fills. Practice playing the roll across different parts of the drum kit, such as snare, toms, and cymbals.

Why Master the Single Stroke Roll?

- **Coordination and Control**: The Single Stroke Roll develops hand coordination and strengthens the ability to play evenly with both hands.

- **Speed and Fluidity**: It helps drummers increase speed and play with greater fluidity, essential for playing faster beats and complex fills.

- **Foundational Rudiment**: As one of the 40 essential rudiments in drumming, mastering the Single Stroke Roll opens the door to more advanced techniques and rhythmic patterns.

11.Double Stroke Roll

The **Double Stroke Roll** is another foundational rudiment in drumming, consisting of two strokes per hand: a **right- right (RR)** or **left-left (LL)** stroke. It is one of the most important rudiments for building speed, control, and endurance, and it forms the basis for more advanced drumming techniques. The Double Stroke Roll is commonly used in drum solos, drumlines, and in creating smooth, fluid rhythms.

Characteristics of the Double Stroke Roll

- **Notation**: The Double Stroke Roll is represented by two consecutive strokes per hand. Each hand alternates between two strokes (right-right or left-left).

- **Duration**: Played continuously with alternating **two strokes per hand** (right-right, left-left) for as long as needed or for the designated number of beats.

- **Role in Rhythm**: The Double Stroke Roll is ideal for creating smooth, flowing patterns and is used for building speed and endurance. It adds a rich, resonant sound to drumming, especially when played with controlled dynamics.

How to Play the Double Stroke Roll

- **Hand Alternation with Two Strokes**: Begin by playing **two strokes with the right hand (RR)** followed by **two strokes with the left hand (LL)**. Continue this alternating pattern (RR LL) for the length of the roll.

- **Even Strokes**: Focus on playing each stroke with equal force, ensuring that both strokes in each hand are balanced in volume and consistency.

- **Relaxed Grip**: Keep your grip relaxed and avoid tension in your hands and wrists. The stick should bounce   naturally with each stroke, allowing for a smooth flow.

- **Stick Height**: Ensure that the rebound height of your sticks remains consistent, allowing for an even sound with each set of strokes.

Practical Exercises

- **Slow and Steady Practice**

Start at a slow tempo, playing two strokes per hand (RR LL) with a focus on evenness and control. Play at a comfortable pace to build accuracy.

Example: Play the Double Stroke Roll for one or two measures, ensuring that each stroke is clear and consistent.

- **Increase Speed Gradually**

Once you are comfortable at a slow pace, gradually increase the tempo while maintaining evenness between the two strokes of each hand.

Work on gradually playing faster while retaining clarity in each set of strokes.

- **Accent Practice**

Practice accenting certain strokes within the Double Stroke Roll to create dynamic variation. For example, accent every first stroke of each hand (Right-Right, Left-Left).

Example: Accent the first stroke of each hand and play the rest of the strokes softer to develop control over dynamics.

- **Double Stroke Roll on Drums**

Practice the Double Stroke Roll on different parts of the drum kit, such as the snare drum, toms, and bass drum. This helps improve your coordination and control while integrating the roll into practical drumming scenarios.

Example: Play the roll on the snare, then move to the toms, ensuring that each stroke remains even across all drums.

Why Master the Double Stroke Roll?

- **Speed and Endurance**: The Double Stroke Roll builds speed and stamina, making it easier to play fast and fluid rhythms over extended periods of time.

- **Control and Precision**: It improves hand control, ensuring that both hands move evenly and with precision, which is crucial for maintaining rhythm and consistency.

- **Versatility**: The Double Stroke Roll is used in many styles of drumming, including rudimental drumming, drumlines, and drum solos. It's a vital tool for developing versatility as a drummer.

12. Paradiddle

The **Paradiddle** is one of the most essential and versatile rudiments in drumming. It consists of a combination of single and double strokes in a specific alternating pattern: **right-left-right-right (RLRR)** or **left-right-left-left (LRLL)**. This rudiment is fundamental for building speed, coordination, and control between the hands and is used in countless musical genres, from rock to jazz to marching percussion.

Characteristics of the Paradiddle

- **Notation**: The Paradiddle is made up of four strokes. The first stroke is a single stroke (right or left), followed by two consecutive strokes with the same hand, and finished with a single stroke with the opposite hand. It can be written as: **RLRR** (Right-Left-Right-Right) or **LRLL** (Left-Right-Left-Left).

- **Duration**: The Paradiddle can be played as a continuous pattern or over a set number of beats. It is commonly played in 4/4 time, but can also be adapted to different time signatures.

- **Role in Rhythm**: The Paradiddle is crucial for improving hand independence, creating smooth and fluid rhythmic patterns, and adding complexity to drum beats and fills.

How to Play the Paradiddle

- **Right-Left-Right-Right Pattern (RLRR)**: Start by playing **Right (R)** followed by **Left (L)**, then two consecutive **Right (R)** strokes. This creates a **RLRR** pattern.

- **Left-Right-Left-Left Pattern (LRLL): Alternatively, play Left (L) followed by Right (R), then two consecutive Left (L) strokes. This creates a LRLL pattern.**

- **Even Strokes:** Focus on maintaining even strokes and ensuring that the rhythm remains smooth between the hands.

- **Relaxed Grip**: Keep your grip relaxed, allowing for natural stick rebound. Tension in the hands and wrists can slow down your playing and affect the quality of the strokes.

- **Consistent Timing**: Play each stroke in time with the beat. The paradiddle should be evenly spaced and fluid, with no rush or hesitation between the strokes.

Practical Exercises

- **Slow Practice**
  Start by playing the **RLRR** or **LRLL** pattern slowly, making sure that each stroke is clean and evenly spaced. Focus on accuracy and control as you build the foundation for faster speeds.

- **Speed Development**
  Gradually increase the tempo once you are comfortable with the pattern. Maintain consistency and clarity as you play faster, ensuring that each stroke remains evenly spaced.

- **Accent Practice**
  Practice accenting different strokes within the paradiddle to develop dynamic control. For example, you could accent the first stroke of each set (RLRR), or the second stroke (LRLL), and play the rest softer. This adds variation and expressiveness to the pattern.

- **Paradiddle Variations**
  Once comfortable with the basic paradiddle, try playing paradiddles in different combinations of hands, such as **RLRL** or **LRLR**, or create longer patterns by combining paradiddles with other rudiments.

- **Apply on Drum Kit**
  Integrate the paradiddle into basic drum kit beats or fills. For example, you can play the **RLRR** pattern on the snare drum while adding bass drum notes on the downbeats. This will help develop coordination between the hands and feet.

Why Master the Paradiddle?

- **Hand Independence**: The Paradiddle improves hand independence by requiring you to alternate strokes with both hands, helping you play more complex rhythms with ease.

- **Coordination and Control**: It strengthens hand control and coordination, which is vital for developing precision in your drumming.

- **Versatility**: The Paradiddle is one of the most commonly used rudiments in drumming. It is highly versatile, making it useful across various musical styles, whether you're playing a basic rock groove, a jazz drum solo, or a marching band cadence.

13. Quaver Note Rest – (Eighth Note Rest)

A **Quaver Note Rest** (also known as an **Eighth Note Rest**) is a musical symbol that indicates a period of silence lasting for the duration of one-eighth of a whole note (or half a quarter note). In drumming, it is used to represent the absence of a stroke or sound for one-eighth of a beat.

In simple terms, a quaver rest tells the drummer to pause for a brief moment, half the length of a quarter note, before continuing with the next stroke. Understanding and incorporating rests is just as crucial as playing notes because it adds rhythmic variety and control to your drumming, allowing the music to "breathe."

Notation of the Quaver Rest

- **Symbol**: The quaver rest is represented by a symbol that looks like a small "7" or a backward "S" placed on the staff, specifically on the space or line where the rest occurs.

- **Value**: It holds the value of one-eighth of a whole note, which is equivalent to half of a quarter note. In time signatures like 4/4, a quaver rest takes up half the time of a quarter note rest (which lasts for one beat).

How to Play with Quaver Rests in Drumming

- **Understanding the Rest**:
  The quaver rest indicates a brief moment of silence in the music, lasting for half the duration of a quarter note. In 4/4 time, it occupies one-half of a beat.

- **Counting the Rest**:
  When you encounter a quaver rest, you must count the silence, just as you would count a note. For example, in 4/4 time, you would count: "1 & 2 & 3 & 4 &", where the rest occurs on one of the "&" counts.

- **Pausing for the Rest**:
  When you see a quaver rest in the music, pause your hands (or foot for bass drum) for the duration of that rest. Ensure that your movement is relaxed and your focus remains on the next stroke or note.

- **Integrating with Strokes**:
  A common practice is to alternate between playing strokes and taking quaver rests, helping you maintain a steady rhythm. For example, you might play a **quaver note** (eighth note) on the snare drum, followed by a **quaver rest**, and then play another quaver note. The challenge is to make sure the rest is just as clean and exact as the stroke.

Practical Exercises

- **Slow Practice with Quaver Rest**:
  Start by practicing a simple pattern, such as alternating between a quaver note and a quaver rest. For example, play a snare hit, then rest, then a snare hit, and so on. Begin slowly to develop precision and timing.

  Example: Play **R - Rest - L - Rest** (Right – Rest – Left – Rest) slowly, ensuring that the rest is of equal duration to the note.

- **Increase Speed Gradually**:
  Once comfortable with the slow pace, gradually increase the tempo. Ensure that you maintain control over the rest, counting it precisely.

  Example: Try increasing the tempo using a metronome while continuing to alternate between snare hits and rests.

- **Quaver Rest in Rhythmic Patterns**:
  Practice adding quaver rests to existing drumming exercises or rudiments. For example, try a basic pattern like **RLRR** (Single Stroke Roll) with alternating quaver rests between each stroke.

  Example: Play **R - Rest - L - Rest - R - Rest - R** in a continuous flow.

- **Apply in Drum Kit**:
  Practice playing the quaver rest across the drum kit by incorporating it into your regular beats. For example, you could add quaver rests in between the snare and bass drum strokes or on the hi-hat to create more dynamic rhythms.

  Example: In a simple rock beat, try alternating between the snare and the bass drum while inserting quaver rests on the hi-hat.

Why Master the Quaver Rest?

- **Timing and Precision**: Mastering the quaver rest helps develop a sense of timing, as you learn to pause for exactly the right amount of time between strokes.

- **Musical Expression**: The quaver rest allows for more expressive drumming by creating space and rhythmic variation. It's essential for shaping the overall feel and dynamics of a piece.

- **Coordination**: Incorporating rests into your drumming improves coordination between your hands and feet, as you learn to control both the strokes and the moments of silence.

14. Basic Rock Beat

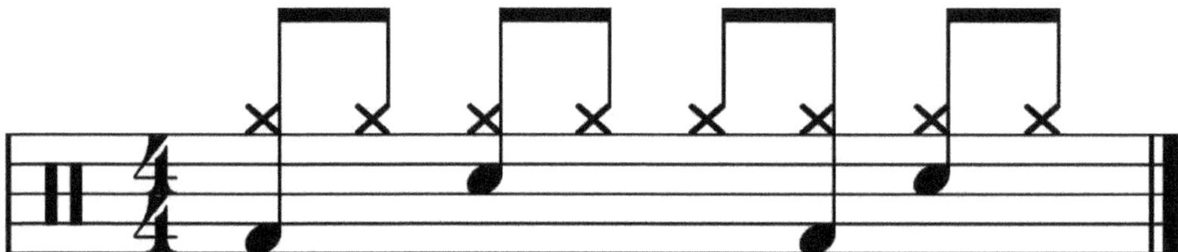

The **Basic Rock Beat** is one of the most fundamental drumming patterns and serves as the foundation for many popular rock, pop, and other genres of music. It's widely used in a variety of songs and is the cornerstone for building your drumming skills. Mastering this beat is essential for every drummer, as it introduces the fundamental coordination between the bass drum, snare drum, and hi-hat cymbals.

Structure of the Basic Rock Beat

The **Basic Rock Beat** typically follows a 4/4-time signature, with the beat broken down as follows:

- **Hi-hat**: Played on every quarter note (beats 1, 2, 3, and 4). In more advanced variations, you might play eighth notes on the hi-hat, but for the basic rock beat, we stick to quarter notes.

- **Bass Drum**: Played on beats 1 and 3. This provides the backbone of the rhythm.

- **Snare Drum**: Played on beats 2 and 4. These "backbeats" create the groove and give the beat its characteristic pulse.

Notation of the Basic Rock Beat

In 4/4 time, the notation would look like this:

- **Hi-hat**: x - x - x - x (played on every beat)
- **Bass Drum**: o - - - o - - - (played on beats 1 and 3)
- **Snare Drum**: - - o - - - o - (played on beats 2 and 4) This can be summarized in a simple pattern: **1 (Bass) - 2 (Snare) - 3 (Bass) - 4 (Snare)**

How to Play the Basic Rock Beat

- **Hi-hat**:
  Play the hi-hat with the right hand (for right-handed drummers), keeping a steady quarter-note pulse. This is often the foundation of the beat. Start slowly and focus on keeping the hi-hat sound clean and even.

- **Bass Drum**:
Use your right foot to play the bass drum on beats 1 and 3. The bass drum gives the beat its pulse, so it's important to keep these strokes consistent and on-time.
Focus on pressing the pedal evenly, ensuring that the sound is not rushed or delayed.

- **Snare Drum**:
Use your left hand (for right-handed drummers) to play the snare drum on beats 2 and 4. This is where the "backbeat" comes in, creating the dynamic "pulse" of the rock rhythm.
Ensure that the snare strokes are clean and hit with a consistent force.

> **Basic Rock Beat Pattern (in 4/4 Time) Count**: 1 - 2 - 3 - 4
> **Hi-hat**: x - x - x - x
> **Bass Drum**: o - - - o - - -
> **Snare Drum**: - - o - - - o -

How to Practice the Basic Rock Beat

- **Start Slowly**:

Begin by playing the beat slowly, ensuring that each component (hi-hat, bass drum, and snare) is clean and precise. Focus on maintaining a steady tempo, even if it's at a slower speed.

- **Use a Metronome**:

Practice with a metronome to ensure that your timing is accurate. Start at a comfortable speed (e.g., 60-70 beats per minute) and gradually increase the tempo as you become more comfortable.

- **Focus on Coordination**:

The key to mastering the basic rock beat is coordination between your hands and feet. Start by practicing one component at a time: first the hi-hat, then the bass drum, and finally add in the snare. Once each limb is comfortable with its part, start playing them together.

- **Incorporate Dynamics**:

Experiment with playing the snare and bass drum with different dynamics, such as playing the snare a little softer or the bass drum a little louder. This adds variety to the rhythm and helps develop control over your drum kit.

- **Add Variations**:

Once you're comfortable with the basic rock beat, try adding in some variations. For example, play eighth notes on the hi-hat instead of quarter notes, or add some fills at the end of the pattern.

Why Master the Basic Rock Beat?

- **Foundation for Many Styles**:

  The basic rock beat is the building block for many different drumming styles and is used in countless rock, pop, blues, and funk songs. Mastering this pattern is essential for any drummer.

- **Improves Coordination**:

  Playing the basic rock beat requires coordination between your hands and feet. It helps build the coordination and independence needed to play more complex rhythms and fills.

- **Versatility**:

  Once you've mastered the basic rock beat, you can easily add more complexity by incorporating different variations, fills, or groove elements, making it a very versatile rhythm.

- **Musical Foundation**:

  A solid understanding of the basic rock beat gives you a strong foundation for developing your drumming skills, making it easier to play with other musicians and develop your own unique drumming style.

15. Backbeat

Simple Backbeat Rhythm

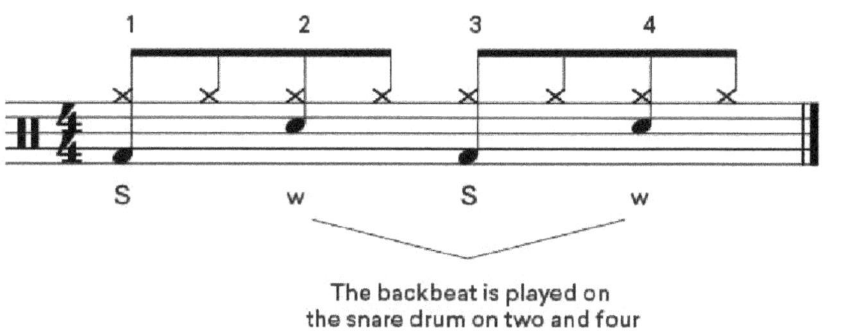

The **Backbeat** is a crucial element in many popular music genres, especially in rock, pop, and blues. It refers to the emphasis placed on the second and fourth beats of a 4/4-time signature, often played on the snare drum. The backbeat provides a strong rhythmic pulse, helping to create the groove that drives the music forward.

Understanding the Backbeat

In a typical 4/4-time signature, the **backbeat** occurs on beats 2 and 4. While the bass drum provides the foundation on beats 1 and 3 (known as the "downbeats"), the snare drum played on beats 2 and 4 (the "upbeats") creates the characteristic "groove" of the music.

Notation of the Backbeat

In a basic 4/4 rhythm, the notation would look like this:

- **Hi-hat**: x - x - x - x (played on every beat)
- **Bass Drum**: o - - - o - - - (played on beats 1 and 3)
- **Snare Drum (Backbeat)**: - - o - - - o -
  This gives us the classic backbeat pattern:
  1 (Bass) - 2 (Snare/Backbeat) - 3 (Bass) - 4 (Snare/Backbeat)

How to Play the Backbeat

- **Hi-hat**:
Play the hi-hat on each quarter note (beats 1, 2, 3, and 4) with your right hand, providing a steady and consistent pulse. The hi-hat serves as the backbone of the beat, maintaining time and keeping the rhythm steady.

- **Bass Drum**:
The bass drum is played on beats 1 and 3, providing a foundation and emphasizing the "downbeats." Use your right foot to press the pedal, making sure that the bass drum strokes are clean and on-time.

- **Snare Drum (Backbeat)**:
The snare drum is played on beats 2 and 4. These "backbeats" are what define the characteristic feel of rock and pop music. Use your left hand to strike the snare drum, ensuring that the backbeat is strong and clear.

  - **Backbeat Pattern (in 4/4 Time)**
  - **Count**: 1 - 2 - 3 - 4
  - **Hi-hat**: x - x - x - x
  - **Bass Drum**: o - - - o - - -
  - **Snare Drum (Backbeat)**: - - o - - - o –

How to Practice the Backbeat

- **Slow Practice**:
Start by practicing the backbeat slowly. Focus on getting a clean, consistent sound from each drum. Begin by playing just the hi-hat and bass drum, then add the snare for the backbeat once you are comfortable with the timing.

- **Use a Metronome**:
Practice with a metronome to help develop a steady sense of timing. Start at a slower tempo (e.g., 60-70 BPM) and gradually increase the speed as you become more confident.

- **Focus on Snare Control**:
The snare backbeat is key to this rhythm, so practice hitting the snare drum with the appropriate force and at the correct time. The backbeat should be prominent and accentuated without overpowering the rest of the beat.

- **Counting Aloud**:
While playing, count the beats aloud to ensure you're playing the backbeat in the correct place. For example, say "1 (bass) - 2 (snare) - 3 (bass) - 4 (snare)" as you play. This helps reinforce the feel of the backbeat.

- **Add Variations**:
Once you're comfortable with the basic backbeat pattern, you can try adding different dynamics or variations. For example, you could play the snare backbeat softer or accentuate the bass drum more. This adds variation to the rhythm while keeping the backbeat intact.

Why Master the Backbeat?

- **Essential Groove**:
The backbeat is a vital part of creating a solid groove. It's the rhythmic element that helps define many styles of popular music, including rock, pop, blues, and funk. Mastering the backbeat allows you to lock in with other musicians and maintain a consistent groove.

- **Timing and Coordination**:
Playing the backbeat requires good coordination between your hands and feet. By practicing this rhythm, you develop better control over your limbs, improving your overall timing and consistency.

- **Musical Feel:**
  The backbeat adds a sense of "push" or "drive" to the music. It is integral to the feel of the song, creating excitement and energy. When executed well, the backbeat can give the music a strong sense of forward motion.

- **Versatility:**
  While the backbeat is often associated with rock and pop, it is also present in many other genres like funk, R&B, and even jazz. Understanding the backbeat allows you to adapt to a wide variety of musical contexts.

Practical Exercises for the Backbeat

- **Basic Backbeat Practice:**

  Begin by playing a simple 4/4 beat, with the bass drum on beats 1 and 3, and the snare on beats 2 and 4. Keep the hi-hat steady and use a metronome to ensure accurate timing.

- **Increase Tempo Gradually:**

  Once you're comfortable at a slower speed, gradually increase the tempo. Maintain steady control over the snare backbeat and ensure that the bass drum doesn't rush or fall behind.

- **Apply the Backbeat to Songs:**

  Try playing along with songs that use a strong backbeat. Start with simpler rock or pop songs that emphasize beats 2 and 4. This will help you internalize the rhythm and develop a better sense of timing in real musical situations.

- **Backbeat Variations:**

  Practice accentuating the backbeat in different ways, either by playing it softer or louder, or by adding ghost notes (quiet, subtle snare hits) in between the main backbeat strokes.

"When you approach this instrument for the first time, what comes out of you is simply what you feel."
– Dennis Chambers

16. Snare Variation

The **snare drum** is one of the most important drums in the drum kit, often used to create accents and rhythms that drive the music forward. A snare variation refers to the different ways the snare drum can be played to create dynamic, interesting rhythms that add complexity and texture to the beat. These variations are essential for any drummer to master as they contribute to the overall feel and groove of a song.

Understanding Snare Variations

Snare variations can include different techniques such as:

- **Accented Snare Strokes**
  An **accented snare stroke** is when you hit the snare drum harder than the regular strokes. Accents are often placed on the backbeat (beats 2 and 4 in a 4/4 measure), but they can also be applied to other parts of the measure to create variation and emphasis.
  Example:
  In a basic 4/4 rhythm, instead of playing the snare at the usual level, you accentuate it on beats 2 and 4 to make them stand out.
  Notation:
  The accented notes are represented by a greater dynamic mark (e.g., > or ^) above or below the notehead.

- **Ghost Notes (Grace Notes)**
  Ghost notes are soft, subtle snare strokes played in between the main beats, typically on the "off-beats" (the "and" counts). They provide texture without distracting from the primary rhythm.
  Example:
  In a standard backbeat pattern, you can add ghost notes between the snare hits on beats 2 and 4 to create a smoother, more intricate groove.
  Notation:
  Ghost notes are usually written with a smaller notehead (e.g., an open notehead or a "grace note").

- **Flams**
  A **flam** occurs when one hand strikes the snare slightly before the other, producing a "graceful" sound. This technique is commonly used to add a dynamic layer to snare strokes, creating a "slap" or "rush" effect.
  Example:
  A flam on beat 2 in a 4/4 rhythm, followed by a normal snare hit on beat 4, creates an off-kilter but exciting texture.
  Notation:
  A flam is notated with a small notehead (for the softer hit) preceding a larger notehead (for the accented hit).

- **Rolls**
  A **roll** is a rapid succession of snare strokes, typically played in quick succession with alternating hands. It can be used to build tension or intensity in music, especially in drum fills or during transitions between sections of a song.

Example:

A **single stroke roll** (alternating between both hands) can be used to create a smooth, rapid sequence of snare hits.

Notation:

Rolls are notated as a series of repeated noteheads, typically with slashes or a "roll" marking above the notes.

- **Snare Off Beats**

  Snare off beats is snare strokes played in between the main downbeats (beats 1 and 3). These offbeat snare variations can add syncopation and surprise to the rhythm, enhancing the groove.

  Example:

  Playing the snare on the "and" of beat 1 or 3 (instead of the typical beats 2 and 4) creates a syncopated rhythm.

  Notation:

  These offbeat snare strokes are notated just like any other snare hit but with the understanding that they fall between the main beats.

Why Snare Variations are Important

- **Adds Complexity**: Snare variations introduce complexity and depth to a drummer's playing, keeping the rhythm from feeling monotonous. They make the drum part more interesting and dynamic.
- **Groove Development**: Many genres of music, particularly funk, jazz, rock, and blues, rely heavily on snare variations to create compelling grooves. A drummer's ability to add and modify snare variations helps maintain the feel of the song.
- **Musical Expression**: Variations in the snare drum part allow the drummer to express emotion and energy in a way that's unique to each song. The snare is a powerful tool for musical expression.
- **Syncopation and Style**: Snare variations are central to creating syncopated rhythms, which are essential in many popular music styles. By playing off-beat snare strokes or using ghost notes, drummers can create intricate patterns that fit the style of the song.

How to Practice Snare Variations

- **Start Slow**:

  Begin practicing snare variations slowly to ensure accurate timing. Focus on getting each variation clear and distinct, especially when incorporating ghost notes or flams.

- **Use a Metronome**:

  Practicing with a metronome will help you develop precise timing for each snare stroke. Focus on maintaining consistent volume for accented notes while keeping ghost notes soft and subtle.

- **Play Along with Songs**:

  Play along with music that includes snare variations to understand how they fit into real-world musical contexts. This will help you develop a sense of timing and how to use snare variations creatively.

- **Combine Variations**:

  Once you are comfortable with individual snare variations, combine them in a single drum pattern. For example, you can add flams to the backbeat, mix in some ghost notes, and play rolls during drum fills.

Practical Exercise

- **Basic Snare Variation Exercise**:
  Practice a simple 4/4 rhythm with the bass drum on beats 1 and 3, and snare variations on beats 2 and 4. Start with a basic snare stroke, then add a flam on beat 2 and ghost notes on beat 4.

  > **Count**: 1 - 2 - 3 - 4
  > **Hi-hat**: x - x - x - x
  > **Bass Drum**: o - - - o - - -
  > **Snare Drum (Variation)**: - - o (accented flam) - - o (ghost note)

Conclusion

Snare variations are essential techniques for any drummer looking to add complexity and flavor to their playing. By mastering various snare techniques such as accents, ghost notes, flams, and rolls, drummers can enhance them rhythmic vocabulary and make their drum parts more engaging. With practice, these variations can become second nature, allowing you to play with more musicality and expression.

17.Cross Stick Technique

Only strike the rim of the pad.

Velocity switching "snare rim" sound, played softly produces a cross stick sound, and when played harder, produces a rim shot sound.

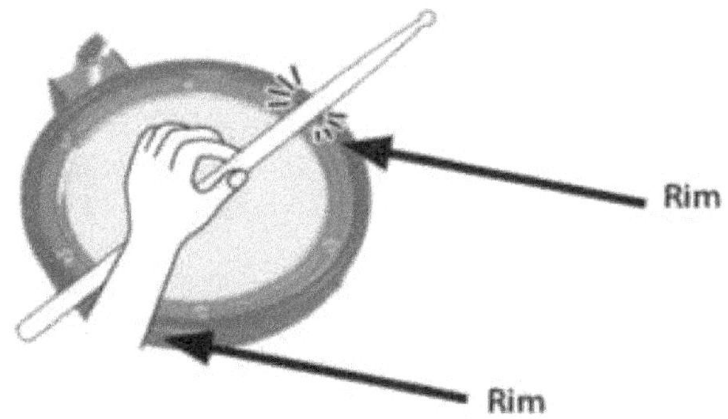

The **cross-stick** technique is an important rhythmic element in drumming that creates a sharp, crisp sound, commonly used in various music genres such as rock, jazz, funk, and Latin. It is a simple but effective technique that involves striking the rim of the snare drum with the tip of the stick while the other end of the stick rests against the snare drum head. The result is a "clicking" sound that is much sharper and brighter than a regular snare hit, making it an excellent choice for creating accents or for providing a distinctive sound in different musical settings.

Understanding Cross Stick

When performing a **cross stick**, the drummer positions the stick horizontally across the snare drum's rim and drumhead. The playing stick's tip is struck against the outer edge of the rim, while the back end of the stick rests on the snare head, creating a unique, percussive "click" sound.

Technique of Cross Stick

- **Positioning the Stick**:

  To perform the cross stick, hold the drumstick normally, but position the tip of the stick across the snare drum's rim. The other end of the stick will rest lightly on the snare drum head.

- **Striking the Rim**:

  The tip of the stick strikes the outer edge of the snare drum's rim while the rest of the stick remains in contact with the drum head. The result is a "clicking" sound that adds a unique rhythmic texture.

- **Control of Sound**:

  The sound of the cross stick depends on the force and angle of the strike. A lighter touch produces a softer, subtler sound, while a firmer strike generates a louder and more defined click.

- **Hand Position**:

While performing the cross stick, it is important to maintain a relaxed and stable grip on the stick. This allows for more control over the tone and ensures the sound is clear and consistent.

When to Use Cross Stick

- **Backbeat Accents**:
  Cross sticks are often used to accentuate the backbeat in a 4/4 rhythm, particularly on beats 2 and 4. The unique sound of the cross stick can provide a refreshing variation from regular snare hits.

- **Light Percussive Textures**:
  Cross sticks are ideal for creating a softer, more textured percussive layer in music. In songs that require a light groove, such as bossa nova or soft rock, cross sticks can add just the right touch without overpowering other instruments.

- **Song Transitions**:
  Cross sticks are often employed in transitions, such as during intros, breakdowns, or the start of a new section, where a change in texture is needed. They can also be used in combination with other snare techniques for contrast.

- **Fills and Breakdowns**:
  Cross sticks can be used effectively during fills and breakdowns, especially when the drummer wants to maintain a rhythmic pulse but not overpower the arrangement with louder snare strokes.

Types of Cross Stick Sounds

- **Standard Cross Stick**:
  This is the most common version, where the drummer strikes the rim of the snare in the middle of the drum with a clean, sharp "click."

- **Light Cross Stick**:
  A softer version where the stick strikes the rim with less force. This creates a delicate, quieter click, perfect for more subtle rhythmic elements or when a lighter texture is needed.

- **Heavy Cross Stick**:
  By striking the rim with more force, this variation produces a louder and more pronounced "click," suitable for more intense passages where you want the cross stick to stand out.

How to Practice Cross Stick

- **Start Slow**:
Begin by practicing at a slower tempo to ensure you are comfortable with the hand positioning and the technique. Focus on hitting the rim squarely with the tip of the stick for a clean sound.

- **Use a Metronome**:
Practice with a metronome to develop accurate timing. Experiment with different tempos and focus on maintaining consistency in both the rhythm and the sound of the cross stick.

- **Alternate Hands**:
Practice cross stick with both hands to build dexterity and comfort. This will also help you in achieving a consistent sound from both the left and right hands.

- **Incorporate Cross Stick into Patterns**:
Start by using cross sticks in simple, familiar patterns like the backbeat in a basic rock groove (on beats 2 and 4). As you get more comfortable, incorporate it into more complex patterns and fills.

- **Combine with Other Techniques**:
Combine cross stick with other snare techniques such as normal snare hits, accents, and rolls. This will give your playing more variety and dynamics.

Practical Exercise

Basic Cross Stick Exercise:
Practice a simple 4/4 rhythm with the cross stick-on beats 2 and 4, while keeping the bass drum on beats 1 and 3.

> **Count**: 1 - 2 - 3 - 4
> **Hi-hat**: x - x - x - x
> **Bass Drum**: o - - - o - - -
> **Snare Drum (Cross Stick)**: - x - x

Notation for Cross Stick

Cross sticks are notated similarly to regular snare hits, but with the addition of a specific mark to indicate the technique. The cross stick is usually represented by a small "X" symbol above the snare note, indicating the drumstick's contact with the rim.

Conclusion

The **cross stick** is an essential technique for any drummer to master. It provides a distinctive percussive sound that can add a new layer of texture to any musical genre. By mastering the cross-stick technique, drummers can enhance their groove, create dynamic rhythmic changes, and contribute to more nuanced and expressive performance.

18. Drum Fills

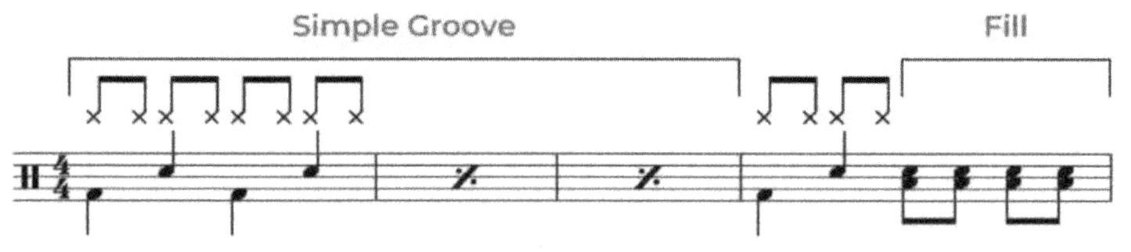

Drum fills are short, dynamic musical passages played between the regular beats of a song, designed to add excitement, transition between sections, or provide emphasis at key moments. They serve as both a rhythmic embellishment and a way to guide the song through changes in mood, tempo, or structure. A well-executed drum fill can make a significant impact, adding flair to the music and enhancing the overall arrangement.

Understanding Drum Fills

A **drum fill** is typically played at the end of a musical phrase or at a transition point, such as before a new section of a song (e.g., from a verse to a chorus). Fills often consist of quick, fluid combinations of beats played across the drums in a creative pattern. They may incorporate snare drums, bass drums, toms, cymbals, and other percussion instruments in various combinations, depending on the style of music and the drummer's personal approach.

Types of Drum Fills

- **Simple Drum Fills**:
  These are short and straightforward fills that usually involve playing a quick snare and bass drum combination, often using the same rhythm from the main beat. They are easy to execute and are commonly used in beginner or basic rock and pop music.

- **Complex Drum Fills**:
  These fills involve more intricate rhythms, incorporating combinations of snare, toms, cymbals, and bass drum in syncopated or polyrhythmic patterns. Complex fills add flair and can be used for dramatic changes in tempo or dynamics. These are common in progressive rock, jazz, and fusion music.

- **Cymbal and Toms Fills**:
  These fills focus on the toms and cymbals. The drummer may play a rolling pattern on the toms followed by a crash cymbal hit, creating a smooth and dramatic transition.

- **Snare and Bass Drum Fills**:
  These fills rely heavily on the snare drum and bass drum, typically alternating between them. It's a great way to drive the rhythm forward, often used in fast-paced rock or metal music.

- **Two-Handed Fills**:
  These involve both hands playing separate rhythmic patterns on different drums, such as playing the snare drum with the left hand and the toms or cymbals with the right. This type of fill can be intricate and fast, adding a greater level of complexity to the overall sound.

- **Roll Fills**:
  These fills involve rapid drum rolls, typically on the snare or toms, to create a buildup of sound before transitioning into another section of the song. The roll can be soft or loud, depending on the desired effect.

Structure of a Drum Fill

- **Timing and Placement**:
  A drum fill typically occurs in the space between two musical phrases, often at the end of a 4-bar or 8-bar phrase. The fill may lead into a new section or mark the end of a musical phrase.

- **Length**:
  Fills can vary in length, ranging from a single measure (one bar) to multiple measures. Shorter fills (one to two beats) are often used for quick transitions, while longer fills (four to eight beats) are used to create a dramatic effect or emphasize a change in the song.

- **Accents**:
  Accents in fills are crucial for adding emphasis to certain beats. A fill can emphasize the downbeat, backbeat, or offbeat to create different rhythmic effects.

- **Dynamics**:
  The dynamic level of a fill is important in determining its impact. A fill can be played softly for a subtle transition or loudly for a more intense shift in the music.

How to Play Drum Fills

- **Start Simple**:
  Beginners should start by practicing simple fills, using basic snare and bass drum patterns. A common fill might involve playing a quick snare hit followed by a bass drum or a tom hit to create a simple transition.
  > Example (in 4/4 time):
  > 1 - 2 - 3 - 4
  > Snare - Snare - Bass Drum – Snare

- **Increase Complexity**:
  As students get more comfortable, they can begin incorporating toms, cymbals, and more complex rhythms into their fills. By adding variations of rhythm and dynamics, they can begin to create more exciting and engaging fills.

  > Example (in 4/4 time):
  > 1 - 2 - 3 - 4
  > Snare - Toms (low, mid, high) - Bass Drum - Crash Cymbal

- **Use the Full Kit**:
  For more advanced fills, try incorporating the entire drum kit: snare, bass, toms, and cymbals. By practicing with all the drums and varying the combinations of hits, drummers can develop their personal style and sound.

- **Practice with Music**:
  The best way to master fills is to practice with actual music. Start by listening to songs and trying to mimic the fills you hear. As you get more comfortable, create your own fills to match the music's energy and feel.

Notation for Drum Fills

Drum fills are notated like regular rhythms, but with the addition of different drum voices (snare, bass, toms, cymbals). Each drum voice has its own notation:

- **Snare Drum**: Typically represented by a note on the middle line of the staff (or above, depending on the positioning).

- **Bass Drum**: Notated on the bottom space of the staff.

- **Toms**: Each tom is typically notated in a separate line or space above or below the snare.

- **Cymbals**: Notated with a specific symbol, typically an "X" for crash or ride cymbals.

Practical Exercise for Drum Fills Basic 4-Bar Fill:
Practice a simple 4-bar fill using just snare and bass drum.

> **Count**: 1 - 2 - 3 - 4
> **Hi-hat**: x - x - x - x
> **Bass Drum**: o - - - o - - -
> **Snare Drum**: - x - - x - x —

Intermediate Fill with Toms:
Move to the toms to create a slightly more advanced fill. Alternate between snare, toms, and bass.

> **Count**: 1 - 2 - 3 - 4
> **Hi-hat**: x - x - x - x
> **Bass Drum**: o - - - - - - -
> **Snare Drum**: - x - - - - - -
> **Toms**: - - x - x - - -

Conclusion

Drum fills are a key element of drumming that adds musicality and dynamic shifts to a song. By practicing different types of fills and varying the complexity of rhythms, drummers can contribute more creatively to the music and enhance the overall listening experience. Mastery of drum fills requires practice and creativity, and it will ultimately help drummers become more expressive and versatile in their performances.

19. Heavy Metal Rock Drumming

Heavy Metal Rock is a genre of music known for its intense, powerful, and aggressive sound. It often features fast tempos, complex rhythms, and energetic performances. For drummers, playing heavy metal rock requires technical skill, endurance, and an understanding of the genre's rhythmic and dynamic characteristics. The drumming in heavy metal is pivotal to driving the powerful energy of the music, with a focus on precision, speed, and aggression.

Characteristics of Heavy Metal Rock Drumming

- **Fast Tempos**:
  Heavy metal rock is typically played at fast tempos, ranging from 120 to 200 beats per minute (BPM). The drummer must be able to maintain consistent speed and control, especially in fast double bass drumming sections.

- **Double Bass Pedal**:
  The **double bass pedal** is a fundamental feature of heavy metal drumming. This technique allows the drummer to play rapid and continuous bass drum patterns using two bass pedals, enabling a more powerful and aggressive rhythm. Double bass is often used in fast breakdowns, blast beats, and high-energy sections of metal songs.

- **Powerful Snare and Bass Drum Hits**:
  Heavy metal drumming focuses on powerful, sharp snare drum hits, often accompanied by strong bass drum strokes. The snare is played with a heavy accent, and the bass drum is used for a driving, deep foundation. The combination of these elements creates the heavy, thunderous sound characteristic of metal.

- **Fast, Complex Rhythms**:
  Rhythmic patterns in heavy metal are often more complex than in other genres. Drummers employ techniques such as **blast beats** (rapid, alternating snare and bass drum strokes), **syncopation**, and **polyrhythms** to create intricate and unpredictable drum parts. Mastering these patterns is key to achieving the signature sound of heavy metal.

- **Ride and Crash Cymbals**:
  Cymbals play a crucial role in heavy metal drumming. The **ride cymbal** is often used to play fast, consistent patterns that help keep time, while the **crash cymbal** is used for accenting key moments in the music, especially during transitions and breakdowns. The high-pitched, sharp sound of the cymbal's cuts through the mix, adding intensity.

- **Syncopated and Offbeat Accents**:
  Syncopation is a prominent feature in heavy metal drumming. Drummers often accent offbeats and utilize ghost notes (soft, unaccented notes) to create rhythmic tension. This adds to the complexity of the drumming patterns, making them feel unpredictable and dynamic.

- **Energy and Aggression**:
  One of the defining characteristics of heavy metal drumming is the level of aggression and energy the drummer brings to the music. This intensity is reflected in the powerful and fast execution of the rhythms, with a constant drive that matches the overall intensity of the genre.

Techniques in Heavy Metal Rock Drumming

- **Blast Beats**:

Blast beats are an essential technique in extreme subgenres of heavy metal like death metal and black metal. This technique involves rapid, alternating strokes between the snare and bass drums. The goal is to achieve a continuous, aggressive rhythm that gives the song a frantic, high-energy feel. Blast beats require precise control and quick footwork.

> Example:
> **Snare Drum**: x - x - x - x -
> **Bass Drum**: o - o - o - o –

- **Double Bass Drumming**:
-

Double bass drumming involves using two bass pedals to create fast and intense bass drum patterns. This technique is commonly used in heavy metal and thrash metal, often played in unison with snare hits to create an overwhelming rhythm section. Drummers use this technique to drive the music forward, especially in fast sections.

> Example:
> **Bass Drum**: o - o - o - o - (left and right bass pedals alternating)

- **Toms and Drum Rolls**:
-

Toms are often used in heavy metal drumming to create rolling fills that add depth and intensity to the music. A tom roll can transition between sections or create dramatic builds within the song. These fills are often played at high speeds, emphasizing the dramatic and energetic qualities of the music.

> Example:
> **Toms**: o - o - o - o - (ascending rolls on the toms)

- **Chops and Rudiments**:

Rudiments such as **paradiddles**, **flams**, and **drags** are frequently applied in heavy metal drumming. These rudiments add speed and complexity to fills and rhythmic patterns. Mastering these techniques is essential for creating fast, intricate drum patterns that define the genre.

Basic Rock and Heavy Metal Beat

While heavy metal drumming often involves complex patterns, it also has a solid foundation in basic rock beats. A typical metal rock beat might involve a steady eighth-note hi-hat pattern with strong backbeats on the snare and driving bass drum patterns. As the genre progresses, drummers often add variations with faster tempos, syncopated accents, and double bass patterns.

Notation for Heavy Metal Rock Drumming

In heavy metal, drummers use standard drum notation, but with additional symbols and techniques. Double bass drumming is represented with two separate bass drum lines, one for each pedal. Blast beats and fast fills are notated using rapid snare and bass drum patterns, often with sixteenth or thirty-second notes to depict their speed.

- **Snare Drum**: Typically notated in the middle or above the staff.
- **Bass Drum**: Notated at the bottom of the staff, with two separate bass lines for double bass.
- **Cymbals**: Notated above the staff, with an "X" used for cymbals.
- **Hi-hat**: Often notated with a simple "x" on the staff.
- **Toms**: Notated in separate lines or spaces, depending on the specific tom used.

Practical Exercise for Heavy Metal Rock Drumming

- **Basic Metal Beat**:
  Practice a basic metal beat with eighth-note hi-hats, strong snare backbeats, and consistent bass drum strokes.

  > **Count**: 1 - 2 - 3 - 4
  > **Hi-hat**: x - x - x - x
  > **Bass Drum**: o - o - - o -
  > **Snare Drum**: - - x - - - x

- **Double Bass Exercise**:
  Practice a simple double bass pattern, alternating between snare and bass drums.

  > **Count**: 1 - 2 - 3 - 4 **Bass Drum**: o - o - o - o **Snare Drum**: - - x - - - -

- **Blast Beat**:
  Practice a basic blast beat, alternating between the snare and bass drums at a fast tempo.

  > **Count**: 1 - 2 - 3 - 4 **Snare Drum**: x - x - x - x **Bass Drum**: o - o - o - o

Conclusion

Heavy metal rock drumming is a dynamic and intense style that demands technical proficiency, speed, and endurance. By mastering essential techniques such as double bass drumming, blast beats, and powerful snare hits, drummers can contribute to the aggressive and fast-paced nature of heavy metal music. With practice, drummers can develop their style and gain the ability to execute complex patterns, creating the intense and energetic rhythms that define the genre.

20. Left Foot Patterns in Drumming

Left Foot Patterns are essential techniques for drummers that enhance the versatility and complexity of drumming in various genres, especially in rock, jazz, and metal. While the right foot typically controls the bass drum (or kick pedal), the left foot is used to operate the **hi-hat pedal**, offering drummers the ability to create additional rhythmic layers and grooves. Mastering left foot patterns can drastically improve coordination, independence, and overall drumming proficiency.

Importance of Left Foot Patterns

- **Improves Coordination**:

Left foot patterns are vital for developing **coordination** between the hands and feet. By practicing complex left foot patterns, drummers can learn to control all four limbs independently, creating more intricate and expressive rhythms.

- **Hi-hat Control**:

The left foot's primary role is to control the **hi-hat** cymbals, typically playing closed, semi-open, or fully open sounds. Left foot patterns can add depth to the groove and provide a strong rhythmic foundation while leaving the hands free to play more complex rhythms.

- **Enhances Groove and Texture**:

The use of left foot patterns can enhance the groove and texture of a song, allowing drummers to create subtle but impactful accents and dynamics. It adds an extra dimension to the drumming by controlling the texture and sound of the hi-hat in conjunction with the rest of the kit.

Common Left Foot Techniques

- **Hi-hat Foot Pedal Closed Sound**:

The most basic use of the left foot in drumming is keeping the **hi-hat cymbals closed** on beats 2 and 4 (in most rock and pop music). This is often referred to as the "backbeat" and provides a driving force in the rhythm.
        Example:
        Count: 1 - 2 - 3 - 4
        Left Foot (Hi-hat): x - x - x - x

- **Open and Closed Hi-hat Patterns**:

Using the left foot, drummers can open and close the hi-hat to create varied textures. **Open hi-hat patterns** allow a more "washy" sound, while **closed patterns** provide a more defined, sharp sound. A combination of these techniques can add excitement and dynamic contrast to the rhythm.

        Example:
        Count: 1 - 2 - 3 - 4
        Left Foot (Hi-hat): o - x - o - x
        (Open hi-hat on beats 1 and 3, closed on beats 2 and 4)

- **Foot Chicks**:

  A **foot chick** is the sound produced when the hi-hat cymbals are slightly open and the left foot presses the pedal to create a sharp, percussive "chick" sound. This technique is often used in jazz, funk, and various other genres to create subtle rhythmic accents.

  > Example:
  > **Count**: 1 - 2 - 3 - 4
  > **Left Foot (Hi-hat)**: (chick) - (chick) - (chick) - (chick)

- **Hi-hat Control for Complex Patterns**:

  Drummers can create **complex patterns** by combining the left foot with hand movements. For instance, the left foot can play alternating open and closed patterns while the hands are busy with complex snare and bass drum combinations. This requires advanced coordination and independence between all four limbs.
  > Example:
  > **Count**: 1 - 2 - 3 - 4
  > **Left Foot (Hi-hat)**: x - o - x — o

Snare and Bass Drum: (Hands playing complex rhythms)

- **Foot Splashes**:

  Foot splashes occur when the left foot rapidly opens and closes the hi-hat in quick succession, producing a short, splashy sound. This technique is used to add accents and flourishes to a beat.

  > Example:
  > **Count**: 1 - 2 - 3 - 4
  > **Left Foot (Hi-hat)**: (splash) (splash) (splash) (splash)

Practical Exercises for Left Foot Patterns

- **Basic Hi-hat Foot Pattern**:

  Start with the basic technique of playing the **closed hi-hat** on each beat to maintain consistent rhythm while keeping time.

  > **Count**: 1 - 2 - 3 - 4
  > **Left Foot (Hi-hat)**: x - x - x — x

- **Hi-hat with Bass Drum**:

  Practice playing the **bass drum** on beats 1 and 3 while keeping the **hi-hat closed** on beats 2 and 4. This exercise builds coordination between the feet and creates a steady rock beat.

  > **Count**: 1 - 2 - 3 - 4
  > **Bass Drum**: o - - o -
  > **Left Foot (Hi-hat)**: x - x — x

- **Foot Chick Exercise**:

Practice the **foot chick** technique by applying the left foot to create a chick sound on every downbeat while playing a steady backbeat on the snare drum.

> **Count**: 1 - 2 - 3 - 4
> **Left Foot (Hi-hat)**: chick - chick - chick - chick
> **Snare Drum**: - x - x –

- **Open and Closed Hi-hat Patterns**:

Create more complex textures by alternating between **open and closed hi-hat** patterns. This will help develop greater foot independence and control.

> **Count**: 1 - 2 - 3 - 4
> **Left Foot (Hi-hat)**: o - x - o - x

Conclusion

Mastering **left foot patterns** is a crucial step toward becoming a more versatile drummer. By controlling the **hi-hat** with the left foot, drummers can enhance their groove, create unique rhythmic textures, and build more complex and dynamic drum parts. As drummers practice left foot.

Snare Drum
Focus on Playing with proper timing and Technique

Anil GT/Sreekumar R Nair

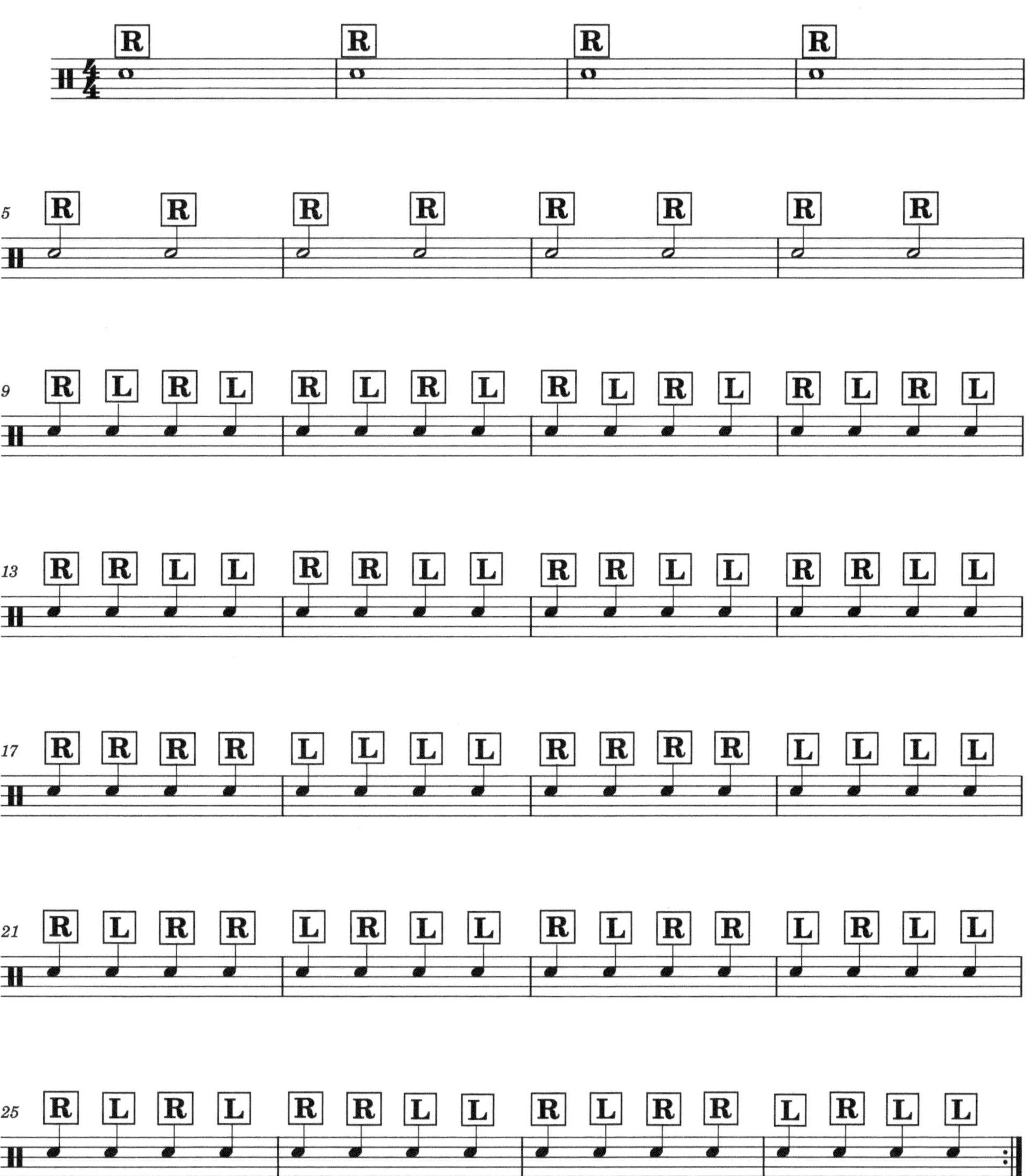

Bass Drum

Foot Position :- Place your foot at the centre of the drum,
with your knee bent at a 90 degree angle

Anil GT / Sreekumar R Nair

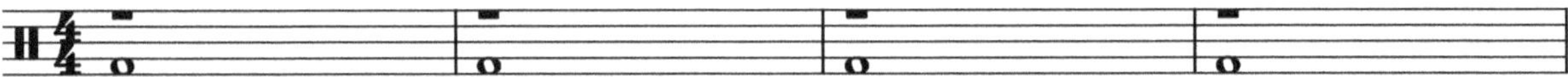

Bass Drum and Snare Drum

Focus on playing with relaxed even feel practice with a to
develop timing

Anil GT / Sreekumar R Nair

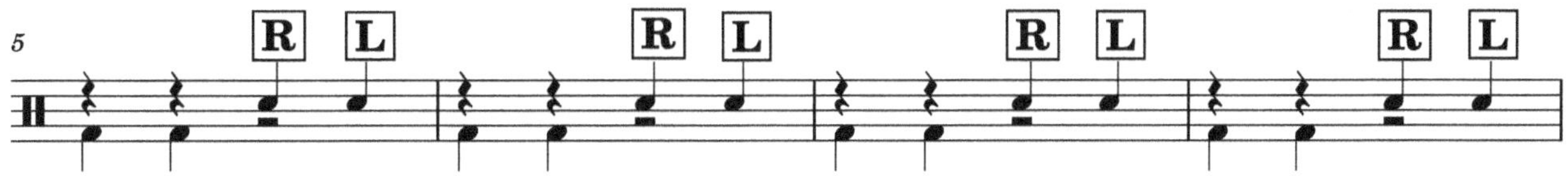

Bass Drum with Snare Drum

Focus on playing with a relaxed, even feel. Practice
with a metronome to develop timing

Anil G T / Sreekumar R Nair

Reading Practice:

Bass Drum, Snare Drum and Hi-Hat

Start with a Simple Groove:
Hi-hat: Play with the tip of the drumstick
Closed hi-hat: Step on the hi-hat Pedal

Anil G T / Sreekumar R Nair

Quaver or Eighth note

A quaver note is musical note that lasts for half a beat.
It is also known as eighth note.

Anil G T/Sreekumar R Nair

Single Stroke Roll

A Single Stroke consists of alternating strokes with each hand,
creating a smooth and even sound.

The basic pattern is: R L R L (or L R L R if starting with the left hand).

Anil G T / Sreekumar R Nair

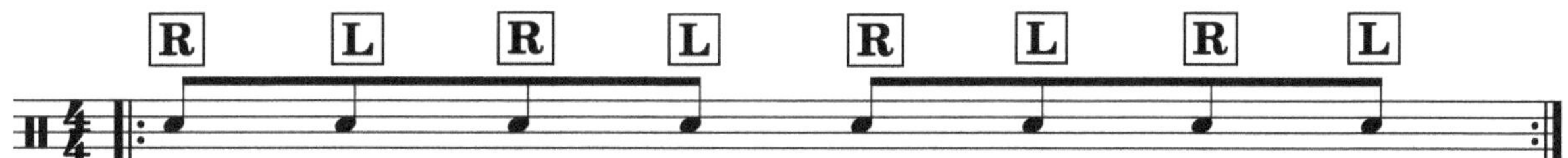

Double Stroke Roll (Mama Dada Roll)

A Double Stroke Roll consists of two strokes with each hand,
creating a smooth, flowing sound.
The basic pattern is: R R L L R R L L

Anil G T /Sreekumar R Nair

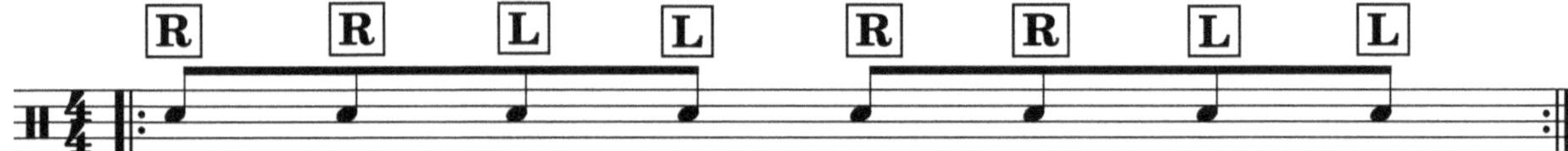

Paradiddle
A Paradiddle consists of the sticking pattern:

R L R R L R L L

It creates a smooth, flowing sound by combining single and double strokes.
Paradiddles are great for developing hand independence, control, and speed.
They also help in transitioning between single and double strokes efficiently.

Anil aG T /Sreekumar R Nair

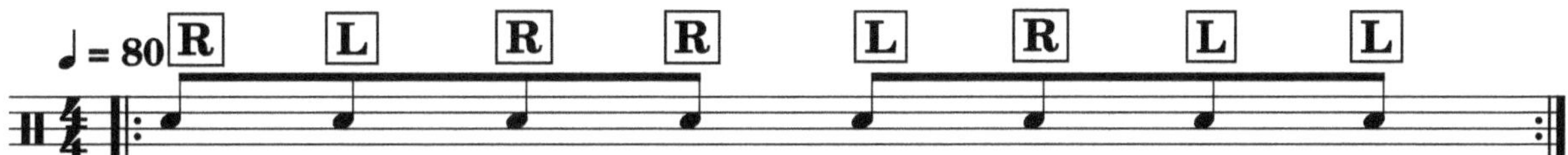

Quaver Rest

A quaver rest is a musical symbol that represents a silence
lasting for half a beat in 4/4 time. It corresponds to the duration of a
quaver (eighth note) but indicates a pause instead of a played note.

Anil G T / Sreekumar R Nair

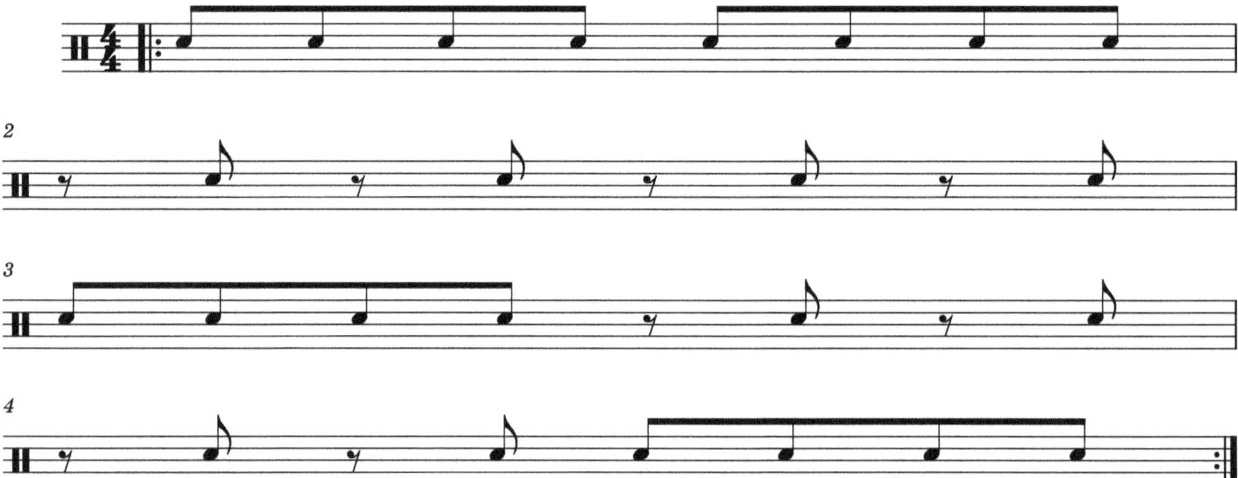

Rock Beat

A rock beat is a fundamental rhythmic pattern in rock music,
typically played in 4/4 time.
It usually features a steady pulse with:

Bass drum on beats 1 and 3
Snare drum on beats 2 and 4
Hi-hat or ride cymbal playing eighth notes

This creates the driving, energetic feel that is characteristic of rock music.

Groove

Groove is used to indicate and underline the rhythmic feel of a song.

Back Beat

The backbeat refers to the strong emphasis on beats 2 and 4 of a measure,
commonly played on the snare drum in rock, pop, and many
other music styles. It creates a driving, rhythmic feel that is essential to
modern popular music, with the snare drum hitting on beats 2 and 4.

Anil GT /Sreekumar R Nair

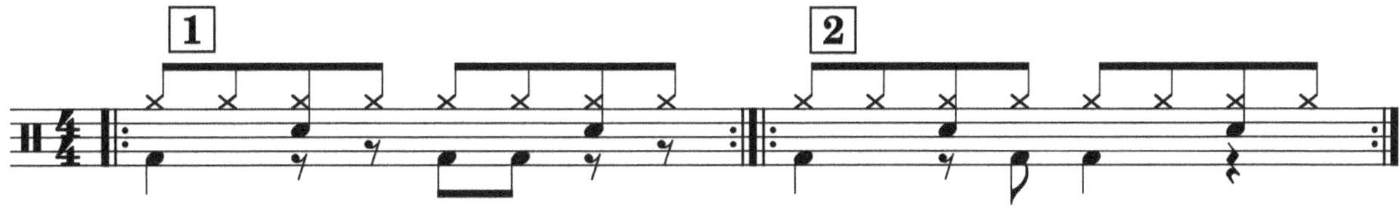

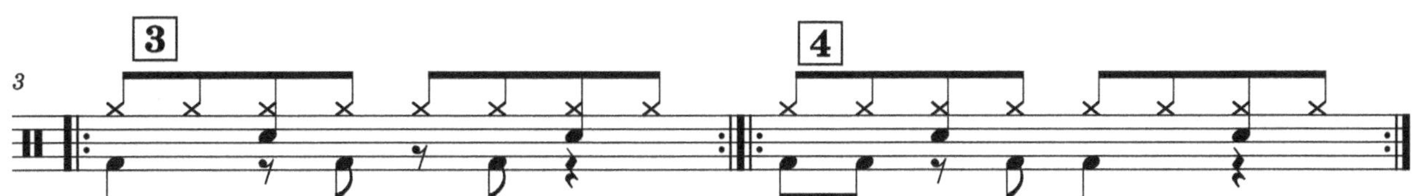

Snare Variation

A snare variation refers to a change or alteration in the
way the snare drum is played, creating a different sound, rhythm, or effect.

Anil G T / Sreekumar R Nair

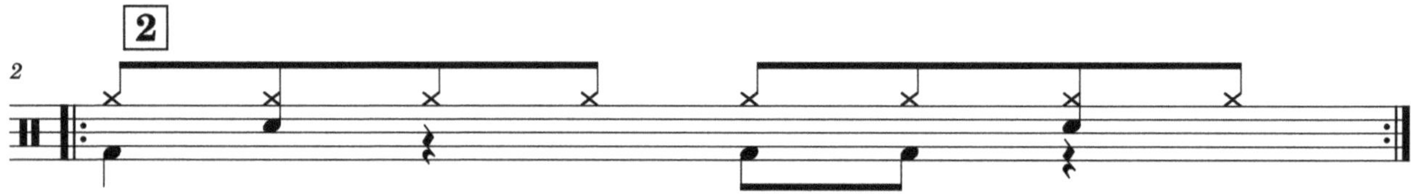

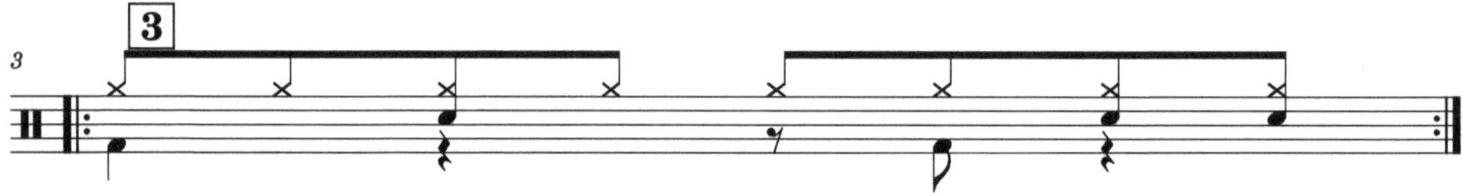

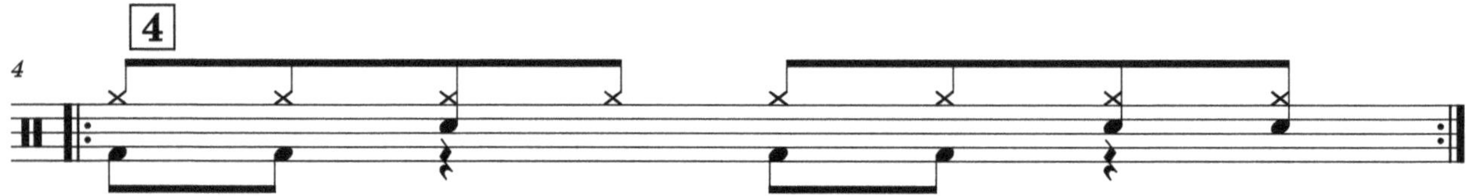

Heavy Metal Rock Beat

A heavy metal rock beat is a powerful rhythmic pattern
commonly used in heavy metal music, often played
using crochet hi-hats or ride cymbals.

Anil G T /Sreekumar R Nair

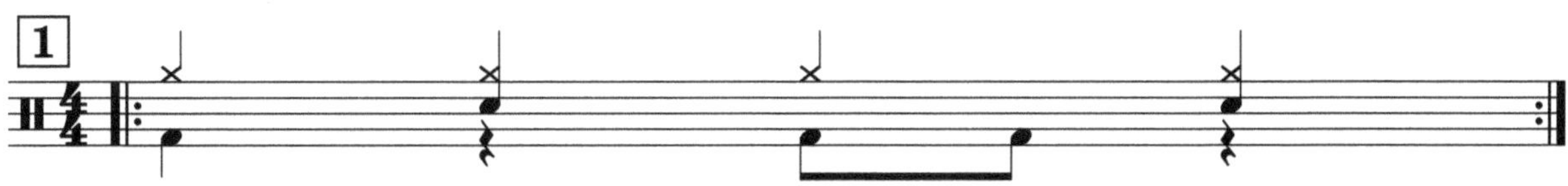

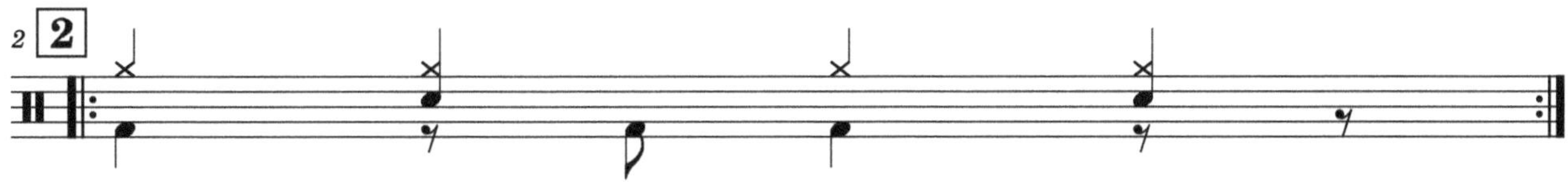

Adding a cymbal

Adding a cymbal improves the beat.

Anil G T/Sreekumar R Nair

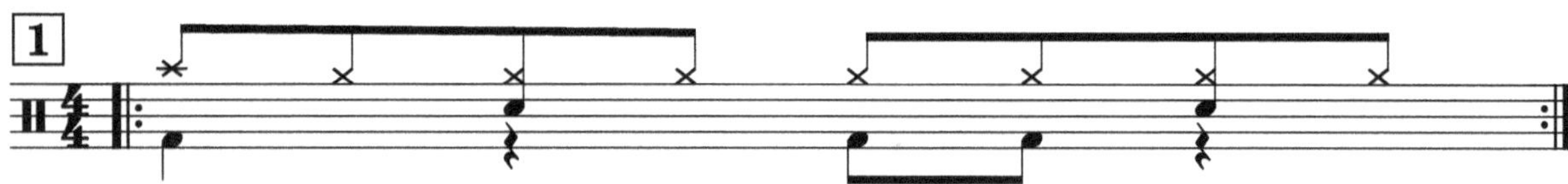

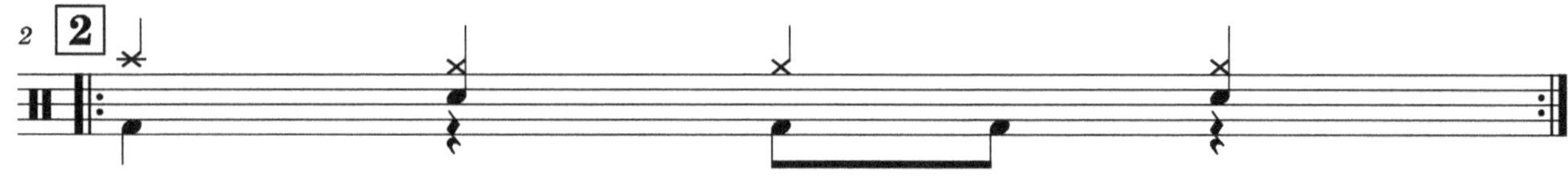

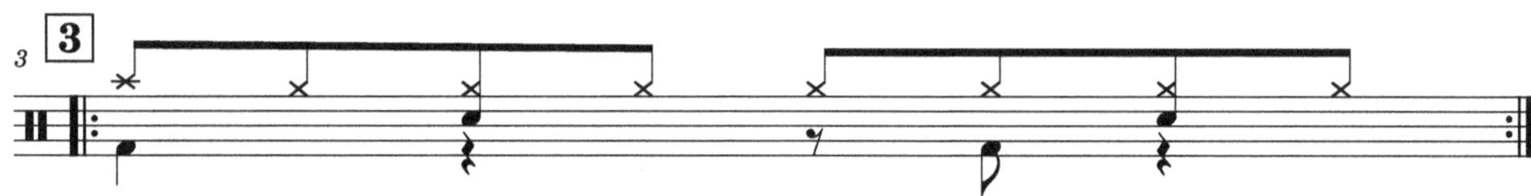

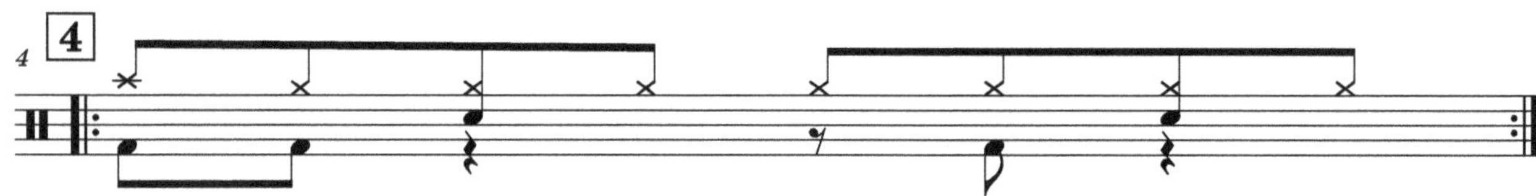

Tom Tom Practice

Tom-Tom practice focuses on developing control, coordination,
and dynamic expression while playing the tom drums.
It enhances a drummer's ability to transition smoothly between
different drums and maintain rhythmic stability. Exercises typically
include single-stroke rolls, double-stroke rolls, paradiddles,
dynamic variations, and fills that integrate toms into drum beats.
Practicing on toms improves hand speed,
accuracy, and muscle memory, making it essential for
various drumming styles, including rock, jazz, and fusion.

Anil G T / Sreekumar R Nair

Drum Fills

Drum fills are rhythmic variations or transitions played between
beats to add excitement and fluidity to a song.
They often involve toms, snare, cymbals, and bass drum, creating dynamic
movement in music. Fills can be simple or complex, using patterns like
single strokes, double strokes, paradiddles, and linear fills.
They help in transitioning between song sections,
adding creativity and expression
to a drummer's performance.

Anil G T / Sreekumar R Nair

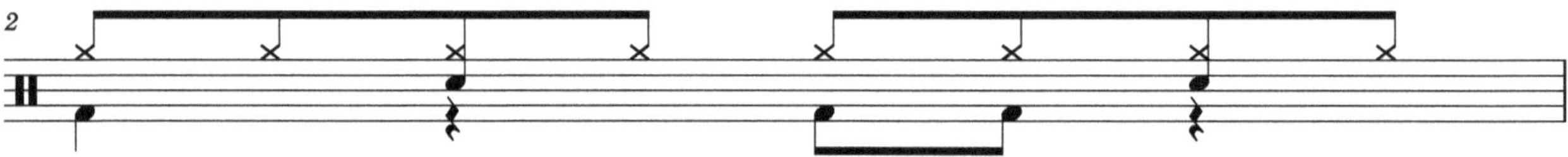

Grade - 1

Table of Contents

1. Semiquaver (Sixteenth Note)

Understanding the Semiquaver (Sixteenth Note) in Drumming

A **semiquaver**, also known as a **sixteenth note** in American terminology, is a short-duration musical note that plays a crucial role in rhythm, groove, and technical development in drumming. It is one of the fastest common subdivisions of a beat, making it essential for creating intricate rhythms, fills, and dynamic grooves across various styles of music.

1. Notation & Time Value

A semiquaver lasts one-fourth of a beat in 4/4 time.

In standard notation, it is represented by a note with a filled-in notehead and two flags (when written individually) or two beams (when grouped with other semiquavers).

Four semiquavers are equivalent to one crotchet (quarter note), two semiquavers equal one quaver (eighth note), and one semiquaver is half of a quaver.

> Example in 4/4 Time: A Single beat (1 count) can be subdivided into four semiquavers:
>
> 1 e & a | 2 e & a | 3 e & a | 4 e & a
>
> This subdivision technique helps drummers maintain precision while playing complex patterns.

2. Role of Semiquavers in Drumming

Semiquavers are fundamental in shaping drumming patterns across different genres, including rock, funk, jazz, Latin, and metal. Their application enhances speed, control, and rhythmic accuracy.

A. Groove Development

Semiquavers are often used in hi-hat patterns to create a fluid groove.

They add depth and variation to beats by introducing syncopation and ghost notes.

Example: Funk and R&B grooves rely heavily on semiquaver hi-hat playing for a smooth, rolling feel.

B. Drum Fills & Rolls

Many drum fills incorporate semiquaver strokes on snare, toms, and cymbals to create flowing transitions between sections of a song. Popular fills include single-stroke (RLRL) and double-stroke (RRLL) patterns in semiquaver subdivisions.

A. Footwork & Bass Drum Independence

In advanced drumming, semiquaver bass drum patterns help develop foot speed and coordination, essential in double bass drumming and intricate Latin rhythms.

Example: Paradiddle-diddle fills use semiquavers to integrate hand-foot combinations smoothly.

3. Techniques to Master Semiquavers

To develop control over semiquavers, drummers should focus on speed, consistency, and dynamic variation through structured practice.

B. Counting Method (Subdivision Awareness)

Saying "1 e & a, 2 e & a, 3 e & a, 4 e & a" out loud while playing helps in internalizing the timing of semiquavers.

Practicing with a metronome at slow tempos before gradually increasing speed improves accuracy.

C. Stick Control Exercises

Practicing rudiments such as single strokes (RLRL), double strokes (RRLL), paradiddles (RLRR LRLL) in semiquaver timing enhances hand speed and endurance.

Dynamics (playing soft and loud) should be incorporated to refine musical expression.

D. Groove & Fill Integration

Alternating between quavers and semiquavers in grooves and fills builds fluency in shifting between note values.

Example:

Basic Beat: | 1 & 2 & 3 & 4 & | (Quaver hi-hats)

Variation: | 1 e & a 2 e & a 3 e & a 4 e & a | (Semiquaver hi-hats)

4. Practical Applications of Semiquavers in Different Styles

Rock & Pop: Used in hi-hats, snare ghost notes, and dynamic fills.

Funk & R&B: Essential for intricate hi-hat grooves and syncopated patterns.

Jazz & Latin: Integral to swing feel and clave-based rhythms.

Metal & Fusion: Applied in double bass drumming for fast-paced rhythms

Conclusion

Mastering semiquavers is crucial for drummers to enhance their timing, groove, and technical proficiency. Through dedicated practice of hand control, foot independence, and groove integration, students at Chempaka Music Academy develop the ability to play with precision and musical expression across various drumming styles.

2. Semiquaver Rest (Sixteenth Note Rest)

Understanding the Semiquaver Rest (Sixteenth Note Rest) in Drumming

A **semiquaver rest**, also known as a **sixteenth note rest** in American terminology, is a musical notation symbol that represents silence for the duration of a **semiquaver (1/16th of a whole note)**. In drumming, understanding and utilizing rests is just as important as playing notes, as they contribute to **rhythmic clarity, groove, and musical expression**.

1. Notation & Time Value

The semiquaver rest has a **curved shape with a hook** (ʾ) and is positioned **above the middle line** of the staff.

It lasts for **one-quarter of a beat** in **4/4 time** (common time).

Four semiquaver rests together equal **one crotchet (quarter note) rest**.

It can appear **individually** or in groups when multiple rests are needed in a measure.

Comparison of Note Durations in 4/4 Time:

Note / Rest	Time Value	Count in a Measure
Semibreve (Whole Note / Rest)	4 beats	1 per measure
Minim (Half Note / Rest)	2 beats	2 per measure
Crotchet (Quarter Note / Rest)	1 beat	4 per measure
Quaver (Eighth Note / Rest)	½ beat	8 per measure
Semiquaver (Sixteenth Note / Rest)	¼ beat	16 per measure

2. Role of Semiquaver Rests in Drumming

In drumming, semiquaver rests **shape the groove and add rhythmic depth** by creating spaces between notes. These brief silences are essential for:

i. Enhancing Groove & Musicality

Rests **separate notes**, allowing grooves to **breathe** and sound more natural.
In **funk and jazz**, well-placed rests create **syncopation and feel**.
Example: A **hi-hat groove** with semiquaver rests can make a pattern more dynamic.

B. Improving Timing & Precision

Practicing with semiquaver rests helps drummers develop a **better sense of timing**.

Rests require **control**—drummers must stop playing at the right moment and resume without hesitation.

C. Creating Syncopation & Complex Rhythms

Syncopation (offbeat emphasis) is achieved by **placing rests on strong beats** or between accents.

Example: A **funk beat** using semiquaver rests makes the groove **tighter and more rhythmic**.

D. Controlling Speed & Dynamics

Using rests effectively prevents **overplaying** and allows for more **dynamic expression**.

Rests in fast fills **break up the flow** and add variation, making patterns more engaging.

3. Practical Application of Semiquaver Rests in Drumming

A. Counting & Subdivision Awareness

To accurately play semiquaver rests, drummers should count and feel the subdivisions.

A **full beat** (one crotchet) subdivided into semiquavers is counted as:

1 e & a | 2 e & a | 3 e & a | 4 e & a

When a semiquaver rest is added, it creates a **gap** in the pattern.

Example 1: Simple Semiquaver Rest Placement

Count	1	e	&	a	2	e	&	a
Hi-hat	X	(Rest)	X	X	X	X	(Rest)	X

Application: This hi-hat groove creates space, adding a crisp, syncopated feel.

B. Groove & Fill Integration

Using semiquaver rests in drum grooves and fills makes patterns sound more **musical and less mechanical**.

Example 2: Funk Groove Using Semiquaver Rests

- Bass drum and snare drum patterns often incorporate semiquaver rests for a "tight" groove.

Count	1	e	&	a	2	e	&	a
Hi-hat	X	X	X	X	X	(Rest)	X	X
Snare	(Rest)	X	(Rest)	X	(Rest)	X	(Rest)	X
Bass	X	(Rest)	X	(Rest)	X	(Rest)	X	(Rest)

Application: This funk groove allows for rhythmic space, making it feel more dynamic.

C. Fills & Soloing

In fills, semiquaver rests **create pauses** that **enhance rhythmic phrasing**.

A common **drum fill with rests** might use **snare, toms, and bass drum** with **pauses for contrast**.

Example 3: Fill with Semiquaver Rests

Count	1	e	&	a	2	e	&	a
Snare	X	(Rest)	X	X	(Rest)	X	X	(Rest)
Tom 1	X	(Rest)	X	X	X	X	(Rest)	X
Bass	(Rest)	X	(Rest)	X	X	X	(Rest)	X

Application: This drum fill is broken up by **rests**, making it sound more intentional and stylish.

4. Techniques for Mastering Semiquaver Rests

A. Slow Practice with a Metronome

Start at **60 BPM**, count **1 e & a**, and place the rests accurately.

Gradually increase tempo for better speed and accuracy.

B. Play with Dynamics & Ghost Notes

Combine rests with **soft ghost notes** for a more expressive groove.

Example: A **ghost note on the snare** after a semiquaver rest adds depth to a funk beat.

C. Syncopation Drills

Practice exercises where rests fall on **strong beats** and **offbeats**.

Example: Snare on **1 & a**, rest on **2**, hi-hat fills the gaps.

D. Apply to Songs & Styles

Listen to funk, jazz, and Latin drummers who **use semiquaver rests effectively**.

Apply these rests in **your own grooves** to make them sound more professional.

5. Practical Application Across Different Genres

Funk & R&B: Syncopated hi-hat and snare drum patterns. **Jazz & Swing**: Creative use of rests in snare and ride cymbal comping. **Rock & Pop**: Strategic pauses in grooves and fills for impact. **Latin & Fusion**: Intricate rest placements in clave-based rhythms.

Conclusion

At Chempaka Music Academy, mastering semiquaver rests is an essential skill for drummers, enhancing timing, groove, and musical expression. By understanding how rests interact with notes, students develop precision and dynamic control in their playing. Whether used in grooves, fills, or solos, effective rest placement adds depth and professionalism to drumming. Through structured practice, drummers learn to create rhythmic contrast, making their playing more engaging and expressive.

3. 2/4 Timing & Drum Fills in 2/4 Time

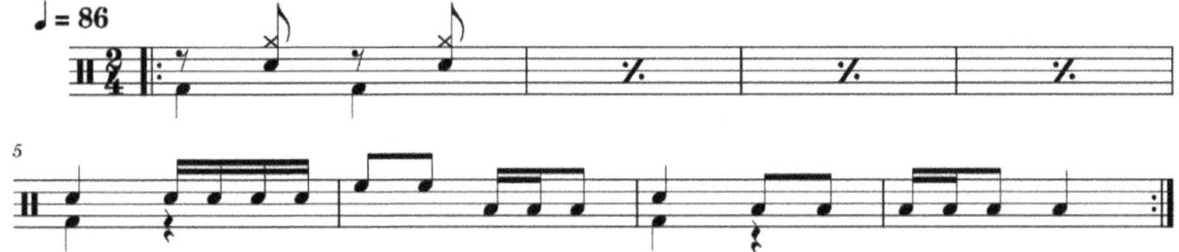

Understanding 2/4 Timing

What is 2/4 Time?

2/4-time signature is a simple duple meter, meaning there are **2 beats per measure**, and each beat is a **crotchet (quarter note)** in duration.

It is commonly found in **marches, polkas, and some fast-tempo grooves**.

The **top number (2)** represents the number of beats in a measure.

The **bottom number (4)** signifies that a crotchet (quarter note) gets one beat.

How to Count 2/4 Time

Since there are only **two beats per measure**, drummers count it as:

"1 – 2 | 1 – 2 | 1 – 2 | 1 – 2"

Subdivisions:

Quavers (eighth notes): "1 & 2 &"

Semiquavers (sixteenth notes): "1 e & a 2 e & a"

Basic 2/4 Drum Beat

Kick on beat 1, snare on beat 2, with a steady hi-hat or ride pattern:

Hi-Hat (or Ride)	x	x
Snare Drum	-	S
Bass Drum	B	-

Count: **"1 – 2 | 1 – 2"**

2. Drum Fills in 2/4 Time

What is a Drum Fill?

A **drum fill** is a rhythmic pattern that adds variation between sections of a song.

In **2/4-time**, drum fills must fit **two beats per measure**, making them quick and impactful.

Fills can use **single strokes, double strokes, tom rolls, or cymbal crashes** to create dynamic transitions.

Basic 2/4 Drum Fill (Single Strokes)

A **simple semiquaver fill** played across the snare and toms:

Snare Drum	R	L	R	L
Tom 1	-	-	R	L
Tom 2	-	-	-	R
Floor Tom	-	-	-	L

Count: **"1 e & a | 2 e & a"**

Advanced 2/4 Drum Fill (Mixed Sticking)

Combining **bass drum, snare, and toms** for a dynamic sound:

Bass Drum	B	-	B	-
Snare Drum	-	S	-	S
Tom 1	-	-	R	-
Tom 2	-	-	-	L

Count: **"1 e & a | 2 e & a"**

3. Practical Exercises for 2/4 Time & Drum Fills

Exercise 1: Basic Groove & Fill (Alternating Measures)

Play a **2/4 groove for three bars.**

On the **fourth bar, insert a semiquaver fill.**

Repeat at different tempos (**60–120 BPM**).

Exercise 2: Syncopated Fill

Mix quavers and semiquavers for variety:

1 & (snare), 2 e & a (toms & bass)

Exercise 3: Marching Style Rudiments

Since **2/4 is common in marching music**, practice rudiments like **paradiddles and flam taps** in this timing.

4. Application of 2/4 in Songs

Marching Bands & Military Drumming: Used in quick-tempo marching beats.

Polka & Folk Music: Dance rhythms often follow a 2/4 feel.

Country & Rockabilly: Certain grooves incorporate 2/4 drum beats for energy.

Conclusion

At Chempaka Music Academy, mastering the 2/4-time signature lays the foundation for precise, dynamic, and controlled drumming. Through structured exercises, students develop essential skills in timing, coordination, and versatility. Focused practice on grooves and short, powerful fills within a two-beat measure builds confidence, enhancing their overall rhythmic proficiency.

4. Two-Measure Combination in 4/4 Time

Understanding Two-Measure Combinations

A **two-measure combination** is a rhythmic pattern that extends across **two full measures (bars) of music**. This concept is widely used in drumming to **enhance phrasing, develop coordination, and create musical variety** in grooves, fills, and transitions.

1. Basics of Two-Measure Combinations

A. Understanding Measures (Bars)

A **measure (bar)** is a segment of music that contains a fixed number of beats, determined by the **time signature**.

In **4/4 time (common time)**, each measure has **four beats**, counted as **1, 2, 3, 4**.

Each **quarter note (crotchet)** gets **one beat**, meaning a two-measure combination consists of **eight beats in total**.

B. Why Use Two-Measure Combinations?

Groove Development: Creates variety by changing the beat slightly between the two measures.

Musical Phrasing: Helps structure a piece of music by organizing rhythmic ideas.

Fill Transitions: Used to move smoothly between different sections of a song.

Improvisation: Encourages drummers to think in **longer phrases**, making playing more expressive.

2. Structure of a Two-Measure Combination

A **two-measure combination** usually follows one of these structures:

A. Identical Measures

Both measures are the **same**, ensuring groove consistency.

Example 1: Basic Two-Measure Rock Groove (4/4 Time)

Count	1	&	2	&	3	&	4	&	1	&	2	&	3	&	4	&
Hi-hat	X	X	X	X	X	X	X	X	X	X	X	X	X	X	X	X
Snare	-	-	X	-	-	-	X	-	-	-	X	-	-	-	X	-
Bass	X	-	-	-	X	-	-	-	X	-	-	-	X	-	-	-

This groove remains **identical across both measures**, making it **steady and reliable**.

B. Variation in the Second Measure

The second measure **changes slightly**, adding variety while maintaining consistency.

Count	1	&	2	&	3	&	4	&	1	&	2	&	3	&	4	&
Hi-hat	X	X	X	X	X	X	X	X	X	X	X	X	X	X	X	X
Snare	-	-	X	-	-	-	X	-	-	-	X	-	X	-	X	-
Bass	X	-	-	-	X	-	-	-	X	-	-	-	X	-	-	-

Example 2: Two-Measure Rock Groove with a Snare Variation

In **measure 1**, the snare plays on beats **2 and 4** (standard rock pattern).

In **measure 2**, an additional snare hit on **beat 3's "&"** adds variation.

C. Fill Leading into the Second Measure

The first measure is a groove, and the second measure includes a **fill**.

Example 3: Groove & Fill Combination

Count	1	&	2	&	3	&	4	&	1	&	2	&	3	&	4	&
Hi-hat	X	X	X	X	X	X	X	X	X	X	-	-	-	-	-	-
Snare	-	-	X	-	-	-	X	-	-	-	X	-	-	X	X	X
Bass	X	-	-	-	X	-	-	-	X	-	-	-	X	-	-	-
Tom 1	-	-	-	-	-	-	-	-	-	-	X	-	-	-	-	-
Tom 2	-	-	-	-	-	-	-	-	-	-	-	X	-	-	-	-

Measure 1 is a groove.

Measure 2 starts as a groove but **ends with a fill** leading into the next section.

3. Benefits of Practicing Two-Measure Combinations

A. Improves Musicality & Flow

Helps drummers **think beyond one bar**, creating more natural grooves and fills.

B. Enhances Timing & Consistency

Strengthens **internal timekeeping** by making drummers aware of longer phrases.

C. Builds Coordination & Endurance

Encourages playing **longer patterns** without stopping, improving **stamina and accuracy**.

D. Develops Creativity in Drumming

Allows for **small variations** within a groove, making playing more **expressive and dynamic**.

4. Practical Applications of Two-Measure Combinations

A. In Rock & Pop Music

Used in **verse grooves** to prevent repetition.

Example: **The second measure may include an open hi-hat or an extra snare hit.**

B. In Jazz & Swing

Ride cymbal and snare comping patterns change subtly over **two bars**.

C. In Funk & Latin Styles

Two-bar grooves often feature **syncopation and ghost notes** for a dynamic feel.

D. In Drum Solos & Improvisation

Helps structure **longer fills and creative phrases**.

5. Techniques to Master Two-Measure Combinations

A. Practice Slowly with a Metronome

Start at **60 BPM**, focusing on accuracy.

Gradually **increase speed** once comfortable.

B. Use Different Time Signatures

Experiment with **3/4, 6/8, and 5/4** for creative phrasing.

C. Apply in Songs

Play along with tracks and **analyse drummer's two-measure patterns**.

D. Record & Listen Back

Identify areas for **improvement in timing and dynamics**.

Conclusion

At Chempaka Music Academy, mastering two-measure combinations is an essential step in developing rhythmic phrasing, coordination, and groove consistency. Whether applied in grooves, fills, or transitions, these combinations help drummers play more musically and naturally. By practicing variations, integrating fills, and applying them across different genres, drummers gain better control, creativity, and versatility in their playing.

"Life is about rhythm. We vibrate, our hearts are pumping blood, we are a rhythm machine, that's what we are."

– Mickey Hart

5. Two Measure Grooves with Fills:

A **two-measure groove with a fill** in **2/4 time** consists of a rhythmic pattern that spans two full measures, where the first measure (or part of the second measure) contains a groove, and the second measure includes a fill. This approach is particularly effective in **fast-paced music genres** such as **marches, polkas, country, rockabilly, funk, and punk rock**, where short and energetic transitions are necessary.

Understanding 2/4 Time Signature

A. What is 2/4 Time?

The top number (2) means each measure contains two beats.

The bottom number (4) indicates that a quarter note gets one beat.

It is counted as 1, 2 | 1, 2, creating a strong downbeat on beat 1 and a lighter beat on beat 2.

B. Difference Between 2/4 and 4/4 Time

Time Signature	Beats Per Measure	Feel & Usage
2/4 Time	2 beats per measure	Shorter, punchy, and energetic
4/4 Time	4 beats per measure	More common in pop and rock, allowing for longer phrasing

2/4 time is ideal for fast-moving, rhythmic music, where quick transitions and fills keep the momentum.

2. Structure of a Two-Measure Groove with a Fill

A two-measure groove with a fill in 2/4 time typically follows this format:

A. Measure 1: Groove

Establishes the foundation of the rhythm with hi-hats, snare, and bass drum.

Maintains a steady pulse to keep the song driving forward.

B. Measure 2: Groove + Fill

The first beat keeps the groove consistent.

The second beat (or second half) is replaced by a fill, adding a dynamic transition.

3. Examples of Two-Measure Grooves with Fills in 2/4 Time

A. Marching Groove with a Snare Fill

Used in marching band and polka-style drumming.

Count	1	2	1	2
Hi-hat	X	X	X	X
Snare	X	-	X	X (fill)
Bass	X	-	X	-

Measure 1: A simple groove with a strong snare hit on beat 1.

Measure 2: Ends with a snare fill, creating a short, punchy transition.

B. Rockabilly Groove with a Tom Fill

Common in rockabilly, punk rock, and country.

Count	1	2	1	2
Hi-hat	X	X	X	-
Snare	-	X	-	-
Bass	X	-	X	-
Tom 1	-	-	-	X (fill)

Measure 1: The groove uses a tight hi-hat and snare on beat 2.

Measure 2: Ends with a tom hit on beat 2, adding a quick transition.

C. Funk Groove with a Ghost Note Fill

Used in funk and jazz-influenced drumming.

Count	1	2	1	2
Hi-hat	X	X	X	X
Snare	-	X	(ghost)	X (fill)
Bass	X	-	X	-

Measure 1: Standard funk groove with a ghost note for feel.

Measure 2: A snare fills on beat 2 to emphasize groove transitions.

4. Why Use Two-Measure Grooves with Fills?

A. Adds Excitement and Momentum

Short fills keep the music moving without breaking the groove.

Essential for high-energy genres that require quick changes.

B. Improves Timing and Coordination

Alternating between groove and fill strengthens internal timekeeping.

Drummers learn to place fills naturally within the rhythm.

C. Enhances Musical Expression

Small variations in fills add uniqueness to a drummer's style.

In genres like punk rock and country, fills define the driving character of the beat.

5. Techniques to Master Two-Measure Grooves with Fills

A. Practice at a Slow Tempo

Start at 60-80 BPM and focus on accuracy.

Gradually increase speed to match the song's tempo.

B. Maintain a Steady Groove

Avoid rushing into the fill—keep the groove solid.

Play along with a metronome or backing tracks.

C. Experiment with Different Fill Variations

Try snare-only fills, tom fills, and bass drum accents.

Create unique combinations based on the style of music.

6. Applications in Different Music Genres

A. Marches & Polkas

Short, repetitive snare fills are crucial for drumline rhythms.

Often played with drum rolls or rudiments.

B. Country & Rockabilly

Hi-hat grooves with snare and tom fills create an energetic bounce.

Works well with train beats and brush drumming.

C. Funk & Punk Rock

Quick syncopated fills maintain the aggressive and groovy feel.

Snare ghost notes and hi-hat variations add depth.

Conclusion

At Chempaka Music Academy, mastering two-measure grooves with fills in 2/4 time is essential for developing control, groove consistency, and musical expression. These patterns are widely used in fast-paced styles, providing energy, momentum, and seamless transitions. By incorporating different fill variations, practicing with a metronome, and experimenting across genres, drummers can refine their technique and enhance their overall musicality.

"Music is the beat of a drum that keeps time with our emotions."
Shannon L. Alder

6. Waltz (3/4 Time):

The **waltz** is a **graceful and flowing musical style** written in **3/4-time signature**, meaning **each measure (or bar) consists of three beats**. It is widely used in **classical music, jazz, folk traditions, and ballroom dance music**. Characterized by its **smooth and elegant rhythm**, the waltz has been a foundational rhythm in Western music for centuries.

Understanding the 3/4 Time Signature

A. What Does 3/4 Time Mean?

The **top number (3)** indicates that **each measure contains three beats**.
The **bottom number (4)** means that a **quarter note** receives **one beat**.
It is counted as: **1 - 2 - 3, 1 - 2 - 3**, forming a repetitive cycle.

B. Strong and Weak Beats in a Waltz
Beat 1 – Strong (accented)
Beats 2 & 3 – Lighter (weaker beats)
This pattern creates the classic waltz "lilt" that gives it a **graceful and swinging feel**.
Example Count:
ONE - two - three | ONE - two - three

2. The Waltz Groove and Feel

A. The Characteristic Waltz Flow

Waltz rhythms are **smooth and continuous**.
The **one-two-three pulse** creates a **circular** and **flowing** movement.
The groove is **gentle yet dynamic**, making it **ideal for dance and lyrical compositions**.

B. How a Waltz is Played on Drums and Other Instruments

Drums – Typically, the **bass drum** or **low tom** plays on **beat 1**, while the **snare drum or hi-hat** marks beats **2 and 3** lightly.
Piano/Guitar – The **left hand (or bass) plays beat 1** (strong), while the **right hand (or chords) plays beats 2 and 3** (lighter).
Orchestral/Band Arrangements – Strings and brass instruments often emphasize the **strong first beat**, creating a **soaring melody**.

Example of a Waltz Drum Pattern:

Count	1	2	3	1	2	3
Bass Drum	X	-	-	X	-	-
Snare/Hi-Hat	-	X	X	-	X	X

3. The Historical Significance of the Waltz

A. Origin in Folk Music

The waltz originated in the 18th century in Germany and Austria, particularly in folk dances.

It became popular in Vienna and spread across Europe.

B. Growth in Classical and Ballroom Music

Johann Strauss II, known as the "Waltz King," composed many famous waltzes, such as *The Blue Danube*.

Waltz music became a dominant ballroom dance rhythm in the 19th century.

4. Playing the Waltz on Drums – The CMA Approach

At **Chempaka Music Academy (CMA)**, the **waltz groove is taught in progressive steps**, focusing on:

A. Mastering the Basic 3/4 Beat

Step 1: Learn the **strong-weak-weak** pattern on the **hi-hat and snare**.

Step 2: Add the **bass drum on beat 1** for emphasis.

B. Adding Variations for Creativity

Introduce **brush drumming techniques** for a **softer waltz feel**.

Experiment with **syncopation and ghost notes** to enhance the rhythm.

C. Improvisation and Style Development

Advanced drummers explore **jazz waltz phrasing**.

Develop **drum fills and transitions** in a 3/4 framework.

6. Common Waltz Drumming Patterns

A. Basic Waltz Beat

Count	1	2	3	1	2	3
Bass Drum	X	-	-	X	-	-
Hi-Hat	-	X	X	-	X	X

B. Jazz Waltz (Swing Feel)

Count	1	2	3	1	2	3
Ride Cymbal	X	(X)	X	X	(X)	X
Snare Ghost	-	X	-	-	X	-
Bass Drum	X	-	-	X	-	-

C. Brush Waltz (Soft & Flowing)

Count	1	2	3	1	2	3
Brush Circles	O	O	O	O	O	O
Bass Drum	X	-	-	X	-	-

Conclusion

At **Chempaka Music Academy**, the **waltz groove is an essential drumming skill,** offering: Improved timing and coordination. Understanding of strong and weak beat placement. Ability to play in different musical styles. Development of dynamic control in drumming.

7. Bossa Nova Groove (Latin Style) in 2/4 and 4/4 Time

Understanding the Bossa Nova Groove

Bossa Nova is a smooth and sophisticated Latin American rhythmic style that originated in Brazil in the late 1950s. A fusion of samba rhythms and jazz harmonies, it is widely used in jazz, samba, and Latin fusion music. The Bossa Nova groove is characterized by its syncopated rhythms, soft dynamic feel, and intricate coordination between the drums, bass, and guitar/piano accompaniment.

- **Origins and Evolution**

  Bossa Nova ("New Wave") was pioneered by Brazilian musicians Joao Gilberto, Antonio Carlos Jobim, and Vinicius de Moraes.

  The style evolved from samba rhythms, but with a softer feel and jazz harmony influences.

- **Bossa Nova's Unique Feel**

  Smooth and flowing rhythm with syncopation.

  Combines Brazilian samba's steady pulse with jazzy harmonic progressions. A laid-back groove, played at moderate tempos (70-120 BPM).

2. Time Signatures in Bossa Nova

A. 2/4 Time Signature

Each measure has two beats (counted 1 & 2 &).

Used in traditional samba-based Bossa Nova grooves.

Creates a light and fast-moving rhythm.

B. 4/4 Time Signature

Each measure has four beats (1, 2, 3, 4).

Most modern Bossa Nova drummers adapt the groove to 4/4, making it more versatile.

Allows for more fluidity and jazz-like phrasing.

3. Groove Structure and Instrumentation

A. Basic Bossa Nova Drum Pattern

Hi-Hat or Ride Cymbal – Plays steady eighth notes to maintain flow.

Snare Drum or Rim Clicks – Plays a syncopated clave-like pattern.

Bass Drum – Replicates the samba-style "heartbeat", alternating between beats.

B. Standard Bossa Nova Drum Notation in 4/4 Time

Count	1 &	2 &	3 &	4 &
Bass Drum	X	-	X	-
Snare (Rim Click)	-	X	-	X
Hi-Hat/Ride	X	X	X	X

The bass drum plays beats 1 and 3, resembling a samba bassline.

The rim click/snare pattern is syncopated, creating the signature Bossa Nova swing.

The hi-hat or ride cymbal plays steady eighth notes, keeping the groove flowing.

C. Samba Influence and Variations

The Bossa Nova groove is derived from the Brazilian samba, which is often played on percussion instruments like the surdo, pandeiro, and tamborim.

In Bossa Nova drumming, the drum kit replaces these percussion instruments while maintaining a similar feel.

4. Bossa Nova in Different Instruments

A. Drums and Percussion

Played on a jazz drum kit, often using brushes or light sticks for a softer sound.

The hi-hat is often played lightly open for a more organic feel.

B. Bass Guitar

Plays a syncopated rhythm, outlining the chord progression.

Usually follows a repetitive "root-fifth" bassline.

C. Guitar and Piano

The guitar plays syncopated chord patterns, using fingerpicking or soft strumming.

The piano plays jazz-influenced harmonies, often voicing extended chords (7ths, 9ths, 11ths, 13ths).

D. Vocals and Melodic Instruments

Bossa Nova vocals are often soft and intimate, emphasizing smooth phrasing.

Instruments like flutes, saxophones, and trumpets are commonly used for melodic solos.

5. Bossa Nova Variations and Styles

A. Traditional vs. Jazz Bossa Nova

Traditional Bossa Nova	Jazz Bossa Nova
Stronger samba influence	More improvisation and swing
Played softly with brushes	Played with sticks for dynamics
Simple chord structures	Complex jazz harmonies

B. Modern Bossa Nova and Fusion

Bossa Nova influences can be found in contemporary jazz, pop, and even electronic music.

Artists like Sting, Sade, and Diana Krall have incorporated Bossa Nova rhythms into their music.

6. How to Play Bossa Nova on Drums – CMA Method

At Chempaka Music Academy (CMA), students are taught Bossa Nova in progressive steps, focusing on:

A. Basic Independence and Coordination

Step 1: Learn the hi-hat eighth-note pulse.

Step 2: Add the bass drum on beats 1 and 3.

Step 3: Introduce the rim click syncopation.

B. Developing Groove Variations

Experimenting with different dynamics.

Playing brush techniques for softer Bossa Nova sounds.

C. Advanced Bossa Nova Concepts

Applying jazz improvisation within the groove.

Mixing Samba elements into Bossa Nova for a hybrid feel.

7. Common Bossa Nova Drumming Patterns

A. Basic 2/4 Bossa Nova Groove

Count	1 &	2 &
Bass Drum	X	-
Snare Rim Click	-	X
Hi-Hat	X	X

B. Extended 4/4 Bossa Nova Groove

Count	1 &	2 &	3 &	4 &
Bass Drum	X	-	X	-
Snare Rim Click	-	X	-	X
Hi-Hat/Ride	X	X	X	X

Conclusion

At Chempaka Music Academy, learning Bossa Nova involves: Developing independence and syncopation. Mastering dynamics and groove control. Applying the groove to different musical styles. Understanding Latin rhythm theory and jazz fusion.

8. 3/4 Funk Groove

Funk is a rhythmically rich, syncopated, and groove-driven style of music that emerged in the 1960s, pioneered by artists like James Brown, The Meters, and Parliament-Funkadelic. It is typically associated with 4/4 time, but 3/4 funk grooves introduce an odd-time phrasing, making them sound unique, dynamic, and complex.

A 3/4 funk groove maintains funk's tight rhythmic structure, syncopation, and ghost notes while adapting to a three-beat pulse. This results in a groove that feels both unconventional and deeply rhythmic, opening new possibilities for drummers, bassists, and rhythm section players.

Understanding the 3/4 Time Signature

A. What is 3/4 Time?

The 3/4-time signature means that each measure contains three beats, and a quarter note gets one beat.

It is commonly found in waltz music, but in funk, it creates a groove with odd phrasing and syncopation.

Unlike 4/4 funk, where backbeats land on beats 2 and 4, 3/4 funk requires creative snare placements and ghost notes.

B. How 3/4 Differs from 4/4 in Funk

Aspect	4/4 Funk Groove	3/4 Funk Groove
Beat Count	4 beats per measure	3 beats per measure
Snare Placement	On beats 2 and 4	Can be placed on beat 2 or shifted
Feel	Linear and continuous	Circular and looping
Groove	Easy to dance to, repetitive	Unconventional, driving and offbeat

1. The Core Elements of a 3/4 Funk Groove

A. Groove Foundation

A solid 3/4 funk groove is built on three key elements:

Steady Hi-Hats – Provide the pulse and drive the rhythm forward.

Syncopated Snare Drum – Accents and ghost notes add funk feel.

Bass Drum Variations – Lock with the bass guitar to create groove depth.

B. Hi-Hat Patterns and Ghost Notes

Tight, closed hi-hats are often played in sixteenth-note subdivisions.

Ghost notes (light snare hits) add dynamics and groove depth.

Funk drumming often features hi-hat openings on offbeats for a signature "chick" sound.

2. Notation and Groove Structure in 3/4 Funk

A. Basic 3/4 Funk Groove Pattern

Count	1 &	2 &	3 &
Bass Drum	X	-	X
Snare Drum	-	X (ghost)	X
Hi-Hat	X	X	X

The hi-hat plays steady eighth or sixteenth notes.

The snare lands on beat 3, with ghost notes on beat 2.

The bass drum locks in with the snare, creating a tight syncopated groove.

B. Variations of the 3/4 Funk Groove

1. Syncopated Bass Drum Groove

Adds extra bass drum hits to create a funkier feel.

Count	1 &	2 &	3 &
Bass Drum	X	-	X
Snare Drum	-	X	X
Hi-Hat	X	X	X

2. Ghost Note-Focused Groove

Uses multiple ghost notes to create a rolling funk feel.

Count	1 &	2 &	3 &
Bass Drum	X	-	-
Snare Drum	(ghost) X	-	X
Hi-Hat	X	X	X

3. Funk Shuffle in 3/4

Swings the hi-hats for a triplet feel.

Count	1 & a	2 & a	3 & a
Bass Drum	X	-	X
Snare Drum	-	X	X
Hi-Hat	X	X	X

4. Key Techniques for Playing 3/4 Funk

A. Ghost Notes & Dynamic Control

Ghost notes are light snare hits that create funk's signature "groove feel."

Played between accented snare hits, adding subtle rhythmic movement. Essential for a tight, funky groove.

B. Syncopation & Groove Flow

Funk thrives on syncopation, meaning accents often fall on offbeats.

Experiment with shifting the snare placement for different groove feels.

C. Hi-Hat Articulation & Openings

Closed hi-hats keep the groove tight and crisp. Occasional open hi-hat accents create a dynamic lift.

Playing sixteenth-note variations can enhance groove complexity.

5. Applying the 3/4 Funk Groove in Music

A. Funk Artists Who Used Odd-Time Grooves

James Brown – Master of syncopation and funk drumming.

The Meters – Groovy, rhythmic funk pioneers.

B. Styles That Use 3/4 Funk

Jazz-Funk & Fusion – Blending jazz improvisation with funk rhythms.

Progressive Rock & Funk – Bands like Rush and Primus incorporate funk in odd-time.

Neo-Soul & R&B – Artists like D'Angelo and J Dilla use syncopation inspired by funk.

6. Learning 3/4 Funk Groove – CMA's Approach

At Chempaka Music Academy (CMA), drumming students are taught 3/4 funk grooves using a structured learning process:

A. Step-by-Step Progression

Step 1 – Mastering basic 3/4-time awareness.

Step 2 – Learning fundamental groove elements (hi-hats, snare, bass drum).

Step 3 – Practicing syncopation and ghost notes.

Step 4 – Developing advanced variations with fills and hi-hat techniques.

B. Focus on Groove & Feel

CMA emphasizes groove over speed, ensuring students develop a deep sense of rhythm. Practice with metronomes, backing tracks, and ensemble play. Incorporating real-world music applications to prepare students for live performance.

Conclusion

A 3/4 funk groove is a unique, syncopated, and deeply rhythmic approach to drumming that challenges traditional funk in 4/4 time. By mastering elements like ghost notes, hi-hat articulation, and bass-snare interaction, drummers can add depth, complexity, and groove to their playing.

9. Swing Style (Latin) Groove

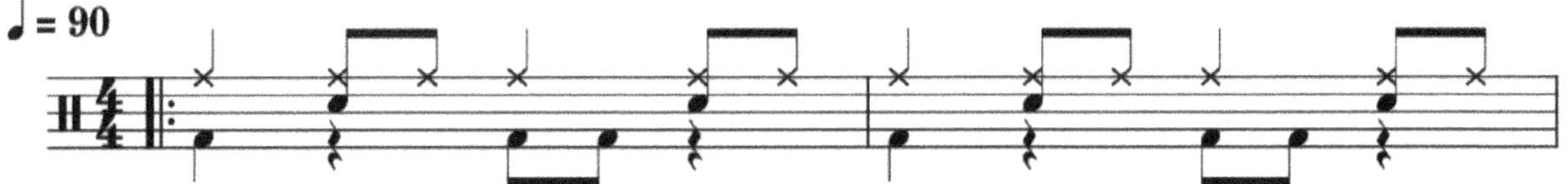

Swing and Latin rhythms are two highly expressive styles in drumming, each with its own unique characteristics: Swing originates from jazz and is based on triplet-based phrasing, creating a laid-back and flowing groove. Latin rhythms derive from Afro-Cuban, Brazilian, and Caribbean traditions, featuring straight, syncopated patterns with complex rhythmic interplay.

A Swing Style (Latin) Groove blends these two styles, creating a rhythm that is both groovy and rhythmically intricate. It retains the triplet-based swing feel of jazz while incorporating syncopated bass drum and snare patterns, hi-hat variations, and ride cymbal interplay from Latin music.

Understanding the Core Elements

A. Time Signature and Feel

Typically, in 4/4, but can also be played in 2/4 (common in samba and bossa nova) or 6/8 (found in Afro-Cuban rhythms).

Swing feel: Emphasizes triplet subdivisions rather than straight eighths.

Latin influence: Incorporates syncopation, clave-based structures, and dynamic interplay between different limbs.

B. Groove Foundation

A Swing Style (Latin) Groove is built on three key elements:

Hi-Hat & Ride Cymbal Interaction – Maintains a triplet-based swing feel or Latin-inspired rhythmic flow.

Syncopated Snare & Bass Drum Patterns – Inspired by Afro-Cuban & Brazilian rhythms.

Clave Structure (Optional) – Many Latin grooves are built around a clave pattern (2-3 or 3-2).

2. The Swing Feel in a Latin Groove

A. Swing vs. Straight Rhythms

Swing uses triplet phrasing, meaning each beat is divided into three equal parts (1-trip-let, 2-trip-let).

Latin grooves are typically straight (evenly spaced notes) but can be adapted to a swing feel by incorporating triplet-based phrasing.

B. How Swing Influences Latin Grooves

The ride cymbal plays a swung triplet pattern similar to jazz drumming.

The snare and bass drum follow Latin rhythmic syncopation, but in a swing phrasing approach.

3. Notation and Groove Structure

A. Basic Swing Style (Latin) Groove in 4/4

Count	1-trip-let	2-trip-let	3-trip-let	4-trip-let
Bass Drum	X	-	-	X
Snare Drum	-	X	-	-
Ride Cymbal	X	-	X	-

Breakdown:

Ride cymbal follows a swing pattern.

Bass drum syncopates in Latin style (similar to song or bossa nova).

Snare drum ghost notes & syncopation add groove depth.

B. Common Variations

1. **2/4 Swing-Latin Groove (For Samba or Bossa Nova Feel)**

Count	1-trip-let	2-trip-let
Bass Drum	X	-
Snare Drum	-	X
Hi-Hat	X	X

2. **6/8 Swing-Latin Groove (For Afro-Cuban Feel)**

Count	1 & a	2 & a	3 & a	4 & a	5 & a	6 & a
Bass Drum	X	-	-	X	-	-
Snare Drum	-	X	-	-	X	-
Ride Cymbal	X	-	X	-	X	-

Breakdown:

This pattern is common in Afro-Cuban 6/8 grooves and blends well with swing triplet phrasing.

The snare drum plays syncopated hits, mimicking Latin percussion instruments.

4. Key Techniques for Playing Swing Style (Latin) Groove

A. Ride Cymbal Articulation

A jazz-style swing ride pattern is essential.

The ride should be played loosely to maintain a natural flow.

Latin variations can add bell accents for a distinct feel.

B. Syncopation & Ghost Notes

Latin music relies on syncopated rhythms, meaning snare and bass hits often fall off the main beats.

Ghost notes (light snare drum taps) create groove depth.

C. Clave Integration (Optional)

If incorporating clave rhythms, the drummer must ensure that the groove respects the clave's phrasing.

Examples:

Son Clave (3-2 or 2-3 pattern)

Rumba Clave (often used in Latin jazz)

5. Application in Different Styles

A. Jazz-Latin Fusion

Found in works by Antonio Carlos Jobim, Tito Puente, and Art Blakey.

Blends bebop swing with Afro-Cuban percussion.

B. Latin Rock & Funk

Used in Santana's rhythms and Herbie Hancock's Latin-inspired grooves.

Often played with funk-style backbeats but Latin bass syncopation.

C. Brazilian Rhythms with Swing Feel

Bossa Nova – A smooth, syncopated groove with a soft swing.

Samba Swing Feel – Faster tempo with rolling hi-hats and syncopated snare work.

Practice Routine:

Start with basic swing ride patterns. Introduce Latin-inspired bass drum placements. Experiment with snare ghost notes and syncopation. Apply grooves to jazz, funk, and Latin music settings.

Conclusion

A Swing Style (Latin) Groove blends triplet-based swing phrasing with Latin syncopation, offering a versatile, rhythmically engaging drumming approach. By combining: Swing's fluid, triplet-based ride patterns, Latin's syncopated snare and bass drum interplay, Clave-influenced groove structures.

"Drumming was the only thing I was ever good at."
John Bonham

Semiquaver

A semiquaver (also known as a sixteenth note in American terminology) is a musical note that lasts for one-sixteenth of a whole note (semibreve).

Anil G T /Sreekumar R Nair

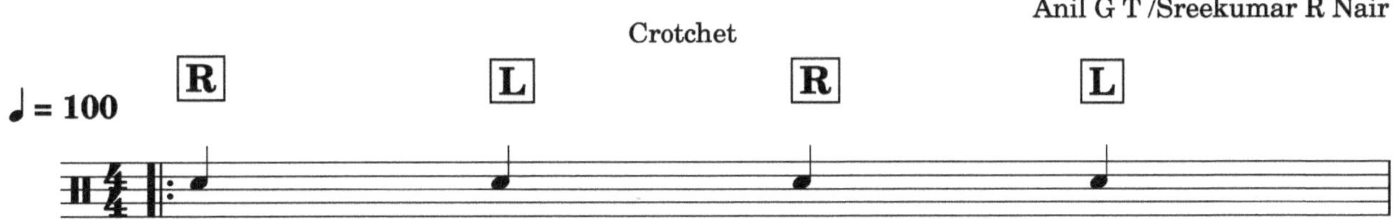

Semiquaver Rest

A semiquaver rest (also called a sixteenth rest in American terminology)
is a musical symbol that represents a silence lasting for
one-sixteenth of a whole note (semibreve).

Anil G T /Sreekumar R Nair

If "e" is a rest in "1 e + a," then you don't need to play it. The correct counting with the rest should be:

"1 (rest) + a"

So, you only play on "1," "+," and "a," while "e" remains silent.

or

If "a" is a rest in "1 e + a", then you don't play it. The correct counting should be:

"1 e + (rest)"

You only play on "1," "e," and "+", while "a" remains silent.

or

If "+" is a rest in "1 e + a", then you don't need to play it. The correct counting with the rest should be:

"1 e (rest) a"

So, you only play on "1," "e," and "a," while "+" remains silent.

or

Shuffled playing session with semiquaver rests"

2/4-Timing
Drum Fills in 2/4 Time

2/4-time signature means two beats per measure,
with a crotchet (quarter note) receiving one beat.

A fill is a short rhythmic break that transitions between sections of a song.
In 2/4 time, fills need to fit within two beats,
so they are typically short and punchy.

Anil G T /Sreekumar R Nair

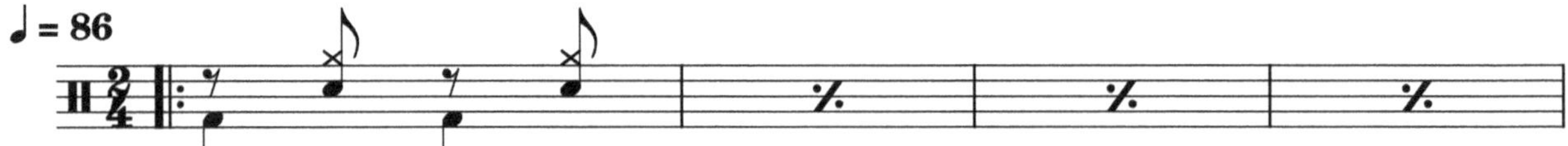

Two-Measure Combination in 4/4 Time

A two-measure combination drum groove is a rhythmic pattern
that spans two measures, creating a sense of continuity and flow.

Anil G T / Sreekumar R Nair

Two Measure Grooves with Fills

A two-measure groove with fills is a rhythmic pattern that spans two measures,
incorporating a drum fill at the end to create a smooth transition.
These grooves help build momentum, variation, and musical expression
in a performance. In 2/4, 4/4, or other time signatures, this approach
adds dynamics and flow, making it essential for various styles like
rock, jazz, funk, punk, country, and pop. Drummers use this technique to
signal transitions, emphasize changes, or enhance the groove in a song.

Anil G T/Sreekumar R Nair

Waltz (3/4 Time)

A waltz is a dance and musical style in 3/4 time, meaning each measure
has three beats (One-two-three, One-two-three).
The first beat is strong, while beats two and three are lighter.

Anil G T /Sreekumar R Nair

Bossa Nova Groove (Latin Style)
in 2/4 and 4/4 Time

Bossa Nova is a Brazilian Latin jazz rhythm that blends
samba with jazz influences. It typically follows a syncopated
groove with a steady bass and offbeat snare or rim clicks.

Anil G T /Sreekumar R Nair

3/4 Funk Groove

Funk grooves are usually in 4/4, but a 3/4 funk groove brings a unique twist!
The key is syncopation, ghost notes, and tight hi-hats
while keeping the groove funky.

Anil G T /Sreekumar R Nair

Swing Style (Latin) Groove

Latin Swing combines the triplet feel of swing with syncopated Latin rhythms.
It blends jazz swing with Afro-Cuban, Brazilian, or Caribbean grooves.

Anil G T /Sreekumar R Nair

Correct Representation of Swing Feel:

☑ Two quavers (♪♪) in swing = A triplet feel (♩♪)

☑ Played as: "Long-Short" instead of "Even-Even"

Comparison:

Straight Quavers: ♪♪ (Evenly played) → "1 & 2 & 3 & 4 &"
Swing Quavers: ♪♪ (Swung feel) → "1 a 2 a 3 a 4 a"
So, in swing rhythm, the first quaver is held longer (like a quarter note),
and the second quaver is played shorter (like an eighth note triplet).

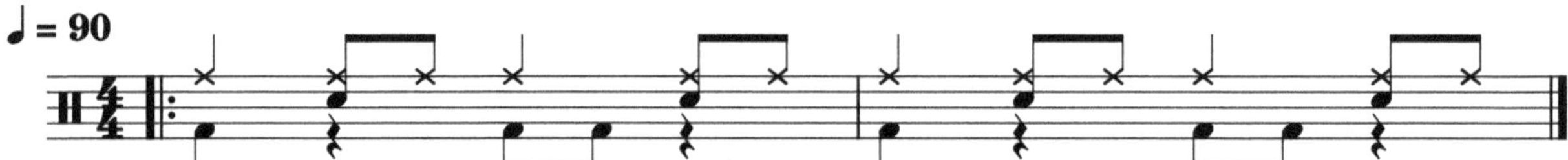

CMA's Drum Groove Practice Session for Students
Groove & Fills

Anil G T /Sreekumar R Nair

Appendices

Glossary of Terms

- **Accent**
  A note played louder or with more emphasis than the surrounding notes.
- **Bass Drum (Kick Drum)**
  The largest drum in the drum kit, played with a foot pedal to produce low-frequency sounds.
- **Beat**
  The basic unit of rhythm, typically felt as the pulse in music.
- **Cymbal**
  A circular percussion instrument made of metal, used to create shimmering, ringing sounds. Examples include crash, ride, and hi-hat cymbals.
- **Drum Kit (Drum Set)**
  A collection of drums and cymbals arranged for a single player to perform.
- **Fill**
  A short drum pattern played between sections of a song, often used as a transition.
- **Flam**
  A rudiment where one stick strikes slightly before the other, producing a "grace note" effect.
- **Floor Tom**
  A larger tom-tom drum that stands on the floor, used for deeper tones.
- **Hi-Hat**
  A pair of cymbals mounted on a stand, played by striking with sticks or using a foot pedal to open and close them.
- **Paradiddle**
  A basic rudiment involving alternating sticking patterns (e.g., RLRR, LRLL).
- **Rimshot**
  A technique where the stick strikes both the drumhead and rim simultaneously for a sharp sound.
- **Snare Drum**
  A drum with wires (snares) stretched across its bottom head, producing a crisp sound when struck.
- **Tempo**
  The speed at which a piece of music is played, usually measured in beats per minute (BPM).
- **Toms (Tom-Toms)**
  Drums without snares, available in different sizes, used for melodic or rhythmic variations.
- **Groove**
  The rhythmic feel or pattern that forms the foundation of a song's rhythm section.
- **Metronome**
  A device or app that produces a steady click to help musicians keep consistent timing.
- **Drumstick**
  A tool used to strike the drum or cymbals, typically made of wood or synthetic material.
- **Polyrhythm**
  The simultaneous use of two or more conflicting rhythms in a musical piece.
- **Practice Pad**
  A portable, quieter surface for practicing drumming techniques and rudiments.
- **Ride Cymbal**
  A large cymbal typically used for steady rhythmic patterns in a song.

2. **Notation Guide**

1. Basic Notation Layout

- **Drum Staff:** Drum notation is written on a single staff (not a grand staff like piano music). Each line and space correspond to a specific drum or cymbal.

2. Common Notation Symbols

Symbol	Instrument	Description
x on the top line	Hi-Hat	Played with a stick; often closed unless otherwise noted.
o on the top line	Open Hi-Hat	The hi-hat is struck while the foot pedal is open.
x above the staff	Ride Cymbal	Played on the ride cymbal; often used for steady rhythms.
x on middle space	Crash Cymbal	Played on the crash cymbal for accentuated sounds.
Notehead (●)	Snare Drum	Played with a stick, located on the second space of the staff.
Notehead (●)	Bass Drum (Kick)	Played with the foot pedal, usually at the bottom of the staff.
Notehead (●)	Toms (Tom-Toms)	Small, medium, and floor toms are placed on different staff lines.
Diagonal Slash	Ghost Note	A softer note played on the snare drum, often part of a groove.

3. Notation Examples

1. Basic Rock Groove

Hi-Hat (x): Steady eighth notes.

Snare (●): Played on beats 2 and 4.

Bass Drum (●): Played on beats 1 and 3.

Notation Example:

x x x x x x x x

●   ●

● ●

2. Snare Roll

A rapid succession of snare drum notes (represented by tremolo slashes above the note).

3. Crash Cymbal Accent

Marked with **x** above the staff and often accompanied by a bass drum hit.

4. Dynamic Markings

- **f (Forte):** Play loudly.
- **p (Piano):** Play softly.
- **Accent (>):** Hit the note with extra force.

5. **Common Time Signatures**

- **4/4:** Most common; four beats per measure, quarter note gets the beat.

- **6/8:** Six beats per measure, eighth note gets the beat.

Books

1. **"Stick Control for the Snare Drummer" by George Lawrence Stone**

   A classic resource for building hand control, speed, and precision.

2. **"Progressive Steps to Syncopation for the Modern Drummer" by Ted Reed**

   Excellent for improving coordination, independence, and syncopation skills.

3. **"Drumset Essentials" by Peter Erskine**

   Covers essential grooves, techniques, and musicality for beginners.

4. **"The Drumset Musician" by Rick Mattingly and Rod Morgenstein**

   Offers a step-by-step guide to learning drum set performance.

5. **"Ultimate Realistic Rock" by Carmine Appice**

   Focuses on rock drumming techniques and rhythms, ideal for modern styles.

Online Resources

1. **Drumeo (www.drumeo.com)**

   Offers structured lessons, practice routines, and expert tips for all levels.

2. **Vic Firth Education Centre (https://ae.vicfirth.com/education)**

   Free lessons, play-along, and exercises by industry professionals.

3. **Modern Drummer Magazine (www.moderndrummer.com)**

   Articles, interviews, and tips from legendary drummers.

4. **Notation and Play-Along Tracks**

   Sheet Music Plus (www.sheetmusicplus.com) for drum sheet music.

YouTube Channels

1. **Drumeo**

   Comprehensive tutorials, tips, and lessons for beginners.

2. **Stephen Taylor**

   Focuses on groove, fills, and improving overall technique.

3. **Mike Johnston**

   Offers lessons on creativity, independence, and applying rudiments.

4. **Drum Channel**

   Features expert interviews, live performances, and masterclasses.

Apps and Tools

1. **GarageBand (iOS)**

   Practice with built-in drum loops and create your tracks.

2. **Drum School (iOS/Android)**

   Offers exercises, grooves, and notation for all levels.

3. **Metronome Apps (e.g., Pro Metronome, Sound Brenner)**

   Essential for practicing timing and rhythm.

Acknowledgements

This guide would not have been possible without the valuable contributions, support, and inspiration from numerous individuals. We extend our heartfelt gratitude to all those who worked tirelessly to breath life in to these pages, especially:

- **The Authors:**

Anil G T (Drum Instructor, Chempaka Music Academy, LCRTC) & Sreekumar R Nair (Programme Coordinator, Chempaka Music Academy, LCRTC)

- **Editor:**

Sreekumar R Nair (Programme Coordinator, Chempaka Music Academy, LCRTC), Jins Thomas, Academic Dean, L`école Chempaka Society for Educare.

- **Guidance and Support**

Chairman	:	**Mr. VNP Raj**
Secretary	:	**Mrs. Sasikala Raj**
Director	:	**Mrs. Sheeja N**
Academic Dean	:	**Mr. Jins Thomas**
CMA Instructor	:	**Mr. John George**
CMA Instructor	:	**Mr. Vivek R S**

(All the Teaching and non-teaching staffs from Chempaka Family)

- **Collaborators**

Chempaka Music Academy, L' école Chempaka Research and Training Centre.

- **Drumming Community**

To the passionate drummers and educators worldwide who inspire beginners and experienced players alike to embrace the joy of drumming.

- ## About Chempaka Music Academy

Chempaka Music Academy (CMA) is the latest endeavor of L'école Chempaka Society for Educare, Trivandrum, an institution that has been synonymous with educational excellence for over four decades. Recognizing the profound impact that quality music education can have on the holistic development of young minds, we have embarked on a journey to integrate music into the educational experience in a truly unique way.

Founded in 2024, under the visionary leadership of Mr. VNP Raj, CMA is dedicated to nurturing the musical talents of students aged 8 to 17. Our academy is committed to providing an enriching and inspiring environment where students can discover, explore, and cultivate their musical abilities.

At CMA, we believe that music is not just an art form but a powerful tool for personal growth, creativity, and academic success. Our curriculum is designed to blend traditional music education with innovative teaching methods, ensuring that every student receives a comprehensive and dynamic learning experience.

- ## Contact Information

Programme Coordinator

Chempaka Music Academy

L'école Chempaka Research and Training Centre

TC 16/3206, "Lekshmi" GG Hospital Road,

Kumarapuram, Trivandrum - 695033

E-mail: officeofrtc@chempaka.org

Contact: +91 9388117035

www.chempakartc.com

www.ingramcontent.com/pod-product-compliance
Lightning Source LLC
Chambersburg PA
CBHW040144110726
48005CB00018B/2636